SHORTCOMINGS

SHORT

NAME: Ben Tanaka
AGE: 30
HEIGHT: 5' 8"
BORN: Corvallis, OR
OCCUPATION: Manager,
University Theater

NAME: Miko Hayashi
AGE: 31
HEIGHT: 5' 4"
BORN: Cambridge, MA
OCCUPATION: Assistant Organizer,
Asian–American Digi–Fest

NAME: Alice Kim
AGE: 29
HEIGHT: 5' 2"
BORN: Incheon, South Korea
OCCUPATION: Graduate Student,
Mills College

ADRIAN TOMINE

SHORTCOMINGS

NAME: Autumn Phelps
AGE: 22
HEIGHT: 5' 7"
BORN: Tacoma, WA
OCCUPATION: Artist/Performer

NAME: Sasha Lenz
AGE: 28
HEIGHT: 5' 8"
BORN: Benicia, CA
OCCUPATION: Graduate Student,
Mills College

NAME: Meredith Lee
AGE: 32
HEIGHT: 5' 5"
BORN: Los Angeles, CA
OCCUPATION: Professor,
New York University

DRAWN AND QUARTERLY, PUBLISHER / MONTREAL

ALSO BY ADRIAN TOMINE

32 Stories: The Complete Optic Nerve *Mini–Comics*

Sleepwalk and Other Stories

Summer Blonde

Scrapbook (Uncollected Work: 1990—2004)

Drawn & Quarterly
Post Office Box 48056
Montreal, Quebec
Canada H2V 4S8
www.drawnandquarterly.com

First hardcover edition: September 2007
Printed in Singapore

10   9   8   7   6   5   4   3   2   1

Library and Archives Canada Cataloguing in Publication
Tomine, Adrian, 1974-
   Shortcomings / Adrian Tomine.
ISBN 978-1-897299-16-6
      I. Title.
PN6727.T65S46 2007   741.5'973   C2007-901244-2

Distributed in the USA by:
Farrar, Straus and Giroux
19 Union Square West
New York, NY 10003
Orders: (888) 330–8477

Distributed in Canada by:
Raincoast Books
9050 Shaughnessy Street
Vancouver, BC V6P 6E5
Orders: (800) 663–5714

Original artwork available at:
www.comicartcollective.com/tomine

FOR SARAH

CHAPTER ONE

FOR MOST OF MY LIFE I HAD FELT DISTANT FROM MY GRANDFATHER, PERHAPS MIS-TAKING THE LANGUAGE BARRIER FOR COLDNESS.

BUT AS I STOOD BESIDE HIM IN HIS AGING FORTUNE COOKIE FACTORY, MY PER-CEPTION OF HIM BEGAN TO CHANGE.

I REALIZED THAT HE WAS VERY MUCH LIKE THE THING HE'D SPENT HIS LIFE MAKING: A HARD, PROTECTIVE SHELL CONTAINING HAIKU-LIKE WISDOM.

KRK

"YOUR LOVE LIFE WILL BE HAPPY AND HARMONIOUS."

CLAP CLAP CLAP CLAP CLAP
CLAP CLAP CLAP CLA

WASN'T THAT FANTASTIC?

LOOK AT ME... I'M CRYING!

MIKO! THANKS SO MUCH. CAROL SAID SHE COULDN'T HAVE DONE IT WITHOUT YOUR HELP.

OH, SHE DESERVES ALL THE CREDIT.

NOW DON'T BE MODEST. WE'LL SEE YOU AT THE BAR IN, SAY... HALF AN HOUR?

I DON'T KNOW IF I'M GONNA MAKE IT. I SHOULD PROBABLY GET MY BOYFRIEND TO BED.

OH, COME ON! I THINK WE ALL DESERVE A DRINK OR THREE. *HA HA*

WELL... I'LL TRY.

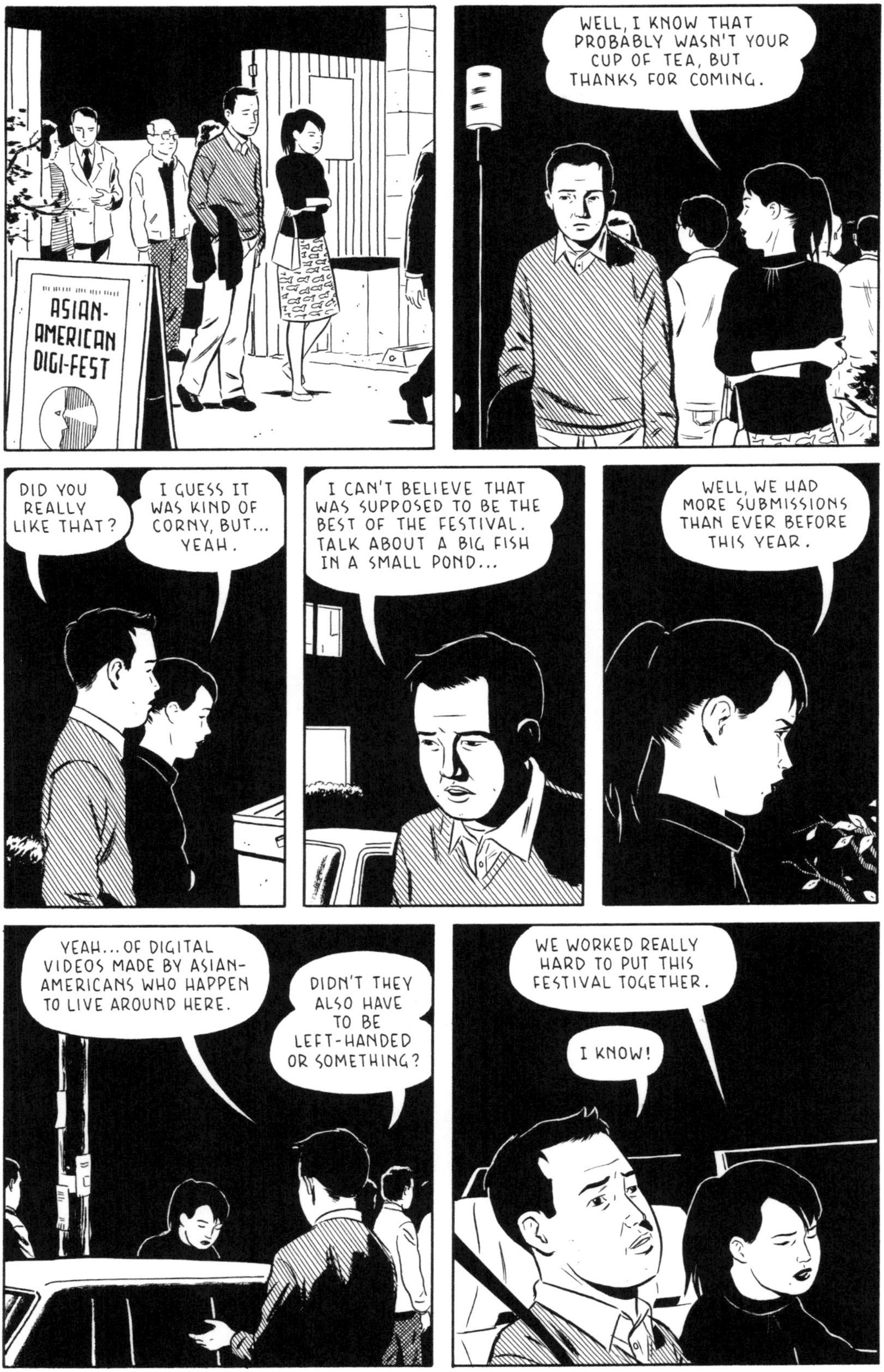
ASIAN-AMERICAN DIGI-FEST
WELL, I KNOW THAT PROBABLY WASN'T YOUR CUP OF TEA, BUT THANKS FOR COMING.
DID YOU REALLY LIKE THAT?
I GUESS IT WAS KIND OF CORNY, BUT... YEAH.
I CAN'T BELIEVE THAT WAS SUPPOSED TO BE THE BEST OF THE FESTIVAL. TALK ABOUT A BIG FISH IN A SMALL POND...
WELL, WE HAD MORE SUBMISSIONS THAN EVER BEFORE THIS YEAR.
YEAH... OF DIGITAL VIDEOS MADE BY ASIAN-AMERICANS WHO HAPPEN TO LIVE AROUND HERE.
DIDN'T THEY ALSO HAVE TO BE LEFT-HANDED OR SOMETHING?
WE WORKED REALLY HARD TO PUT THIS FESTIVAL TOGETHER.
I KNOW!

I'M NOT CRITICIZING *YOU*. I'M CRITICIZING THE SHITTY MOVIE. AM I ALLOWED TO VOICE MY OPINION?

YOU DON'T HAVE TO. YOU MADE IT PERFECTLY CLEAR WITH ALL YOUR FIDGETING AND GROANING.

I'M SURE THAT LING COULD HEAR YOU SNICKER-ING THROUGHOUT HER FILM.

IT'S GOOD FOR HER! YOU CAN'T CONTROL AN AUDIENCE'S REACTION.

WELL, IT'S A LITTLE EMBARRASSING FOR ME. AND REALLY, WHO ARE *YOU* TO CRITICIZE?

HEY...I KNOW A LOT MORE ABOUT MOVIES THAN SHE DOES.

I'M IN THE INDUSTRY...

"THE INDUSTRY"? YOU MANAGE A THEATER!

THAT'S RIGHT...A *REAL* MOVIE THEATER. WHERE NONE OF THOSE MOVIES ARE GOOD ENOUGH TO PLAY AT.

LOOK, IF YOU DIDN'T LIKE THE MOVIE, THAT'S FINE. I DON'T UNDER-STAND WHY YOU HAVE TO GET SO ANGRY.

BECAUSE EVERYONE KNOWS IT'S GARBAGE, BUT THEY CLAP FOR IT ANYWAY BECAUSE IT WAS MADE BY SOME CHINESE GIRL FROM OAKLAND!

I MEAN, WHY DOES EVERYTHING HAVE TO BE SOME BIG "STATEMENT" ABOUT RACE? DON'T ANY OF THESE PEOPLE JUST WANT TO MAKE A MOVIE THAT'S **GOOD**?

GOD, YOU DRIVE ME CRAZY SOMETIMES. IT'S ALMOST LIKE YOU'RE ASHAMED TO BE ASIAN.

WHAT?

AFTER A MOVIE LIKE THAT, I'M ASHAMED TO BE **HUMAN**!

OKAY, LET'S JUST... DROP IT.

:SIGH:

I WAS IN SUCH A GOOD MOOD...

CREPE EXPECTATIONS

I JUST HATE THAT SHE HAS TO TAKE A CONVERSATION ABOUT SOME STUPID MOVIE AND TURN IT INTO A PERSONAL ATTACK ON ME...

"A PERSONAL ATTACK"? GOD...I'M SURE SHE WAS JUST RESPONDING TO YOUR *CHARMING* NEGATIVITY.

WHAT AM I SUPPOSED TO DO...PUT ON SOME CHARADE AND ACT LIKE MY JUDGMENT IS JUST AS CLOUDED AS HERS?

I MEAN, SHE DIDN'T GIVE A SHIT ABOUT ANY OF THIS COMMUNITY... POLITICAL...*WHATEVER* WHEN I MET HER.

YOU'RE SO ARTICULATE WHEN YOU GET INDIGNANT.

OKAY...

CLUB WITH FRIES FOR YOU...

AND YOU'VE GOT THE TOFU SCRAMBLE CREPE.

THANKS.

I LIKE YOUR HAIR. IT'S REALLY CUTE.

REALLY?

I JUST CUT IT MYSELF. I WAS THINKING I SHOULD GO GET IT FIXED.

DO YOU KNOW WHAT KIND OF—

NO WAY!

I SHOULD GET YOU TO CUT *MY* HAIR SOMETIME!

HEY, SORRY TO INTERRUPT BUT...

CAN I JUST ASK... DO YOU KNOW WHAT KIND OF OIL THEY COOK THE FRIES IN?

OIL?

UH, I THINK IT'S CANOLA.

OKAY, THANKS.

WELL, JUST LET ME KNOW IF YOU NEED ANYTHING.

I WILL.

DO YOU KNOW HER?

NOT YET...

ANYWAY...I'M JUST SAYING THAT IT'S MIKO WHO'S CHANGED, NOT ME.

SO SHE'S GOTTEN A LITTLE MORE POLITICALLY-MINDED. I DON'T GET WHY THAT'S SUCH AN AFFRONT TO YOU.

IT'S NOT. IT JUST GETS KIND OF TIRESOME.

I MEAN...MAYBE I'D CARE MORE IF I EVER FELT LIKE I'D BEEN THE VICTIM OF SOME KIND OF...DISCRIMINATION OR SOMETHING, BUT...

YEAH, WELL...YOU LIVE IN, LIKE, THE MOST LIBERAL, DIVERSE CITY IN THE WORLD! YOU'D CHANGE YOUR TUNE IF YOU SUDDENLY FOUND YOUR-SELF IN ALABAMA OR SOMETHING.

I GREW UP IN *OREGON!* I WAS PRACTICALLY THE ONLY NON-ARYAN IN MY ENTIRE SCHOOL!

AND YOU NEVER FELT MISTREATED OR...DISCRIM-INATED AGAINST?

OF COURSE! BUT NOT BECAUSE I WAS ASIAN.

IT WAS BECAUSE I WAS A NERD WITH A BAD PERSONALITY AND NO SOCIAL SKILLS!

YOU MIGHT HAVE A POINT THERE.

REMEMBER THAT GUY FROM THE DORMS... ELVIN...SOMETHING?

ELVIN WANG.

YEAH!

OF COURSE... THE GUY WHO BLAMED ALL HIS PROBLEMS ON RACISM.

EXACTLY! YOU'RE LIKE THE TOTAL OPPOSITE OF HIM. YOU REFUSE TO SEE—

OKAY, OKAY... ENOUGH.

PLEASE.

SO HOW'S SCHOOL? ARE YOU...

THE SAME. I'M NEVER GONNA FINISH.

I TRY TO STUDY, BUT ALL I CAN THINK ABOUT ARE THE INCOMING FRESHWOMYN.

THE WHAT?

THE FIRST-YEAR STUDENTS. THAT'S WHAT THEY'RE CALLED.

ARE YOU SERIOUS?

THAT'S WHAT THEY'RE CALLED.

OKAY, OKAY...

≥SIGH≤ THEY'RE SO CUTE AND NAIVE. MY GOAL IS TO AT LEAST MAKE OUT WITH A HUNDRED GIRLS BY THE TIME I GET MY Ph.D.

JESUS! I TOLD YOU NOT TO GO TO MILLS FOR GRAD SCHOOL. YOU'RE TOO WEAK!

WELL, WE ALL HAVE OUR PRIORITIES...

USED

OPEN

PSSHHH

CAROL THINKS THAT OUR ATTENDANCE MIGHT HAVE ACTUALLY *TRIPLED* THIS YEAR.

WOW.

AND THAT'S IN SPITE OF THE FACT THAT THOSE JERKS AT THE WEEKLY REFUSED TO GIVE US A WRITE-UP.

UH-HUH.

HOW'S ALICE? DID YOU GUYS HAVE LUNCH TODAY?

YEAH. YOU KNOW... SHE'S HER USUAL SELF...

...PURSUING THIS GIRL, SLEEPING WITH THAT GIRL...

I'M STILL WAITING FOR HER TO SHOW UP SOME DAY WITH HERPES ALL OVER HER MOUTH.

IT'LL BE LIKE WHEN MY HIGH SCHOOL GYM TEACHER CAME BACK FROM SPRING BREAK AND SHE HAD ALL THESE—

OKAY... ENOUGH.

MM... THIS LOOKS GREAT.

DID I GET ANY MAIL TODAY?

YOU GOT A PACKAGE. WHAT DID YOU ORDER NOW?

I DON'T KNOW... MORE DVDs. I CAN'T EVEN REMEMBER WHAT MOVIES THEY ARE.

LOOK AT THIS...

THEY CALL THIS AN "IMPROVED DIGITAL TRANSFER"? AND WHERE'S THE GOD-DAMN EXTRAS?

PIECE OF JUNK...

DO YOU WANT TO GO TO BED?

ENH... I'M NOT REALLY TIRED YET. I SLEPT IN TODAY.

WELL, WE DON'T HAVE TO GO TO SLEEP RIGHT AWAY.

MAYBE I'LL COME TO BED IN A LITTLE BIT. I STILL HAVE A COUPLE OTHER DISCS I WANT TO CHECK OUT.

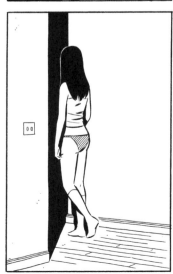

GENE, THIS IS AUTUMN. SHE'S JUST STARTING TODAY.

HI THERE.

OH, HEY. TOP FIVE FAVORITE MOVIES.

UH... WHAT?

I SAID, NAME YOUR TOP FIVE FAVORITE MOVIES. MINE ARE (IN DESCENDING ORDER): FIGHT CLUB, BOOGIE NIGHTS, JAY AND SILENT BOB STRIKE BACK, RESERVOIR DOGS, AND

GENE! LET'S TRY NOT TO SCARE HER OFF ON HER FIRST DAY, OKAY?

YIKES.

YEAH...SORRY. LET ME SHOW YOU HOW THE BOX OFFICE WORKS.

BEEP BEEP

HI! WHAT ARE YOU DOING HERE?

I WENT OUT TO DINNER, SO I ORDERED YOU SOME TAKE-OUT.

WITH WHO? YOU'RE ALL DRESSED UP.

JUST SOME OF THE GIRLS FROM WORK.

HERE...EAT BEFORE THE TEMPURA GETS SOGGY.

THANKS.

I'LL BE HOME AROUND ONE. YOU GONNA BE AWAKE?

I'LL TRY.

SORRY FOR THE INTERRUPTION.

SHE'S PRETTY.

YEAH. WANT SOME?

I'M FINE.

OKAY...I SHOULD TELL YOU THAT WE HAVE A LITTLE VIDEO CAMERA UP THERE, SO YOU'LL KIND OF BE... MONITORED.

I KNOW IT'S PARANOID, BUT...

ARE YOU GONNA BE WATCHING ME?

IT'S NOT THAT I DON'T TRUST YOU. IT'S JUST A THEATER RULE.

OH, I KNOW.

ACTUALLY, I LIKE BEING WATCHED. MY THERAPIST SAYS I'M AN EXHIBITIONIST BY NATURE.

OH... UH-HUH...?

YEAH...YOU SHOULD COME CHECK OUT ONE OF MY SHOWS SOMETIME. I'M PART OF THIS GROUP THAT DOES PERFORMANCE ART, SPOKEN WORD, THAT KIND OF STUFF.

REALLY? LIKE AT CLUBS, OR...?

YEAH... CLUBS, WAREHOUSE PARTIES...

BUT I DON'T KNOW... IT MIGHT BE TOO WEIRD FOR YOU.

WHAT DO YOU MEAN?

NO...THAT SOUNDS GREAT. YOU SHOULD DEFINITELY LET ME KNOW WHEN THAT'S HAPPENING BECAUSE...YEAH.

OH MY GOD... I AM **NOT** GOING TO HAVE THIS ARGUMENT!

IT'S NOT AN ARGUMENT. I'M JUST SAYING THAT I KNOW YOUR TYPE.

NO YOU DON'T, BECAUSE I DON'T **HAVE** A "TYPE."

O-KAY...

DO YOU REALLY THINK I'D BE ATTRACTED TO SOME GRUBBY, PUNK WEIRDO?

OH, DON'T OVERDO IT. SHE'S ALSO CUTE, WHITE, AND I KNOW HOW—

JESUS CHRIST!

YOU JUST *CAN'T* DROP IT, CAN YOU?

WHAT IS SHE... TWENTY? NINETEEN?

I HAVE NO IDEA! BUT IF IT'S SO FUCKING IMPORTANT TO YOU, I'LL BE SURE TO ASK HER!

WELL, I MUST'VE TOUCHED A NERVE.

YEAH...BY INSULTING ME AND, AND... INSTIGATING THIS STUPID *BULLSHIT*!

OKAY, WAIT...

GOD, I'M SICK OF THIS SHIT!

THIS ISN'T GOOD FOR EITHER OF US.

YEAH.

I THINK WE CAN BOTH MAKE AN EFFORT TO NOT LET THESE THINGS GET OUT OF CONTROL.

I KNOW.

LET'S TRY TO SAVE OUR ARGUING FOR SOMETHING REAL, OKAY?

THIS WAS JUST SO... NOTHING.

I DON'T KNOW WHY I KEEP PUSHING YOUR BUTTONS SOMETIMES.

I'M PROBABLY JUST TRYING TO GET SOME KIND OF REACTION OR SOMETHING.

WELL... I GUESS IT WORKED.

TCH... IT'S JUST EMBAR-RASSING.

I MEAN... THAT'S NOT WHO I AM.

I KNOW.

THANKS FOR DOING THIS.

IT'LL GO A LONG WAY TOWARDS KEEPING MY FAMILY IN DENIAL.

DIDN'T YOU ONCE TELL ME SOMETHING ABOUT YOUR PEOPLE HATING MY PEOPLE?

UH... HELLO?

DOES THE PHRASE "WORLD WAR II" RING A BELL WITH YOU? YOUR PEOPLE RAPED AND PILLAGED MY PEOPLE!

OH... THAT.

MY GRANDMA STILL REFUSES TO EVEN EAT AT A JAPANESE RESTAURANT.

STILL, I'M SURE MY FAMILY WOULD RATHER SEE ME WITH A JAPANESE BOY THAN A KOREAN GIRL.

I SEE...

SO RAPISTS AND PILLAGERS ARE PREFERABLE TO HOMOS.

EVERYTHING IS PREFERABLE TO HOMOS.

WHY DON'T WE JUST SAY I'M KOREAN WHILE WE'RE AT IT?

YOU KNOW... REALLY MAKE THEIR DAY.

ALL ASIANS MIGHT LOOK THE SAME TO *YOU*, BUT MY FAMILY WOULD SPOT YOUR JAPANESE ASS A MILE AWAY.

BESIDES... I DON'T WANT TO SATISFY THEM *TOO* MUCH.

25

HOLD MY HAND.

ARE YOU SERIOUS? JESUS, THIS IS—

SHH!

WHAT?

I TOLD YOU... GOOD CHRISTIAN BOYS DON'T TAKE THE LORD'S NAME IN VAIN.

I'M SUPPOSED TO BE CHRISTIAN, TOO? HOW FAR ARE WE TAKING THIS BULLSHIT?

SHH!

MAN...LOOK AT ALL THESE ASIANS!

:SIGH: HERE WE GO...

안녕 앨리스. 늦었네...

HI MOM... HI DAD.

안녕.

이 사람이 그때 말한 그 남자친구야?

UH, YEAH...

MOM, DAD... THIS IS BEN.

HI THERE!

HELLO, BEN. I DIDN'T CATCH YOUR LAST NAME...?

UH... TANAKA.

VERY NICE TO MEET YOU, BEN.

IT'S GREAT TO MEET YOU BOTH!

그 남자가 일본인이란 말이야?

딱 보면 알지, 왜 울라?

이런 뒷담은 안하면 안될까가?

왜, 그런거 물어보면 안되는거냐?

한국인이면 그냥 대놓고 얘기하지.

아이고...흉시나 했더니 역시나... 창피해 더이상 못 참겠다!

WERE YOU GUYS ARGUING, OR IS THAT JUST THE WAY YOUR LANGUAGE SOUNDS?

HEY...I SAID, WERE YOU GUYS ARGUING, OR—

SHUT UP.

ARE YOU OKAY?

I'M FINE.

THANKS FOR DOING THAT.

OH...NO PROBLEM. THANKS FOR COOKING.

I NEED TO TALK TO YOU ABOUT SOMETHING.

UH-HUH...?

I WAS LOOKING FOR SOME STAMPS TODAY AND, UH...

I FOUND THESE IN YOUR DESK.

K-KLAK

Sapphic SORORITY

LOOK...LET'S NOT MAKE A BIG DEAL OUT OF THIS. IF IT BOTHERS YOU, I'LL THROW THEM OUT. I GOT THEM A LONG TIME AGO, AND...

WELL, THE THING THAT KIND OF BOTHERS ME IS THAT ALL THE GIRLS ARE WHITE.

WHAT?

THAT'S NOT TRUE. LOOK...THERE'S A, UH, *LATINA* GIRL IN THIS ONE...

OR WAIT... MAYBE SHE'S ON THE "ALL-GIRL ACTION" DISC. LET ME SEE...

HOW WOULD YOU LIKE IT IF I WAS OBSESSED WITH PICTURES OF BIG, MUSCULAR AFRICAN-AMERICAN MEN?

YEAH, RIGHT... YOU REACH FOR YOUR PEPPER-SPRAY THE MINUTE YOU SEE A BLACK GUY WALKING TOWARDS YOU ON THE STREET!

I'M NOT JOKING AROUND, BEN.

LOOK...THIS STUFF IS JUST, YOU KNOW... FANTASY. IT'S **SUPPOSED** TO BE DIFFERENT FROM REALITY...OTHERWISE, WHAT'S THE POINT?

I MEAN, IF YOU WERE STRANDED ON A DESERT ISLAND, YOU WOULDN'T SIT AROUND DREAMING ABOUT SAND AND SUN, RIGHT?

YOU'RE NOT MAKING THIS ANY BETTER.

NO, LISTEN...

MY POINT IS THAT SAND AND SUN ARE **GREAT**, IT'S JUST—

DO YOU HAVE **ANY** IDEA WHY THIS MIGHT OFFEND ME?

IT'S LIKE YOU'RE OBSESSED WITH THE TYPICAL WESTERN MEDIA BEAUTY IDEAL, BUT YOU'RE SETTLING FOR ME.

JESUS...I'M NOT "SETTLING." WHERE DID YOU GET THIS IDEA THAT A GUY CAN ONLY BE ATTRACTED TO ONE "TYPE"?

WELL, I NOTICE WHAT YOU **GAWK** AT WHEN WE'RE OUT, AND IT'S ALWAYS SOME—

OH MY GOD...

OKAY! SO I'M BRAIN-WASHED BY SOME INSIDIOUS MEDIA CONSPIRACY INTO THINKING THAT BLONDE-HAIRED, BLUE-EYED WOMEN ARE ATTRACTIVE!

WHAT AM I SUPPOSED TO DO ABOUT IT?

YOU'RE A FUCKING ASSHOLE!

WHAT DID I DO? I *SAID* I'D THROW THE DVDs AWAY...

IT'S NOT LIKE I'M CHEATING ON YOU OR SOMETHING. I JUST—

ARE YOU SURE ABOUT THAT?

ARE YOU CRAZY? WHAT THE HELL IS WRONG WITH YOU?

STOP YELLING! WHAT ARE *YOU* GETTING SO ANGRY ABOUT?

BECAUSE YOU ALWAYS ASSUME THE WORST ABOUT ME! YOU NEVER GIVE ME THE BENEFIT OF THE DOUBT, AND YOU'RE ACTING CRAZY OVER NOTHING!

IT'S NOT "NOTHING," AND I'M NOT ACTING CRAZY, SO STOP USING THAT FUCKING WORD!

SLAM!

HEY, BEN...?

JESUS, GENE... HAVE YOU HEARD OF KNOCKING?

UH, LISTEN... AUTUMN WANTS TO RUN NEXT DOOR FOR A BURRITO, BUT IF I COVER FOR HER, THEN I'LL BE LEAVING HUMBERTO ALONE AT THE CANDY COUNTER, AND—

GENE!

I'M SURE HUMBERTO CAN HANDLE IT FOR A FEW MINUTES. TELL AUTUMN TO GO AHEAD.

HUH.

OKAY...

BOX OFFICE

...ANYWAY, THEY'RE TELLING US THAT WE HAVE TO LET THESE SEISMIC RETROFIT GUYS INSPECT THE THEATER, AND **WE** HAVE TO PAY FOR IT!

THAT'S ANNOYING.

S FA GO B

DO YOU REMEMBER THAT INTERNSHIP I APPLIED FOR?

HMM...

THE ASIAN-AMERICAN INDEPENDENT FILM INSTITUTE?

I GUESS NOT. WHAT ABOUT IT?

WELL, I HEARD BACK FROM THEM FINALLY, AND... I GOT IT!

SUS

REALLY? THAT'S GREAT, I GUESS. WHAT DOES THAT MEAN? ARE YOU...?

WELL, THE THING IS... IT'S IN NEW YORK.

WHAT?

YOU DEFINITELY NEVER TOLD ME ABOUT **THIS**.

WELL, IT'S A FOUR MONTH PROGRAM.

FOUR MONTHS? ARE YOU KIDDING ME?

I KNOW...BUT IT'S AN AMAZING OPPORTUNITY.

WELL, FORGET IT.

WHAT ARE YOU TALKING ABOUT?

IT JUST SEEMS LIKE AN AMAZING OPPORTUNITY BECAUSE IT'S IN NEW YORK.

YEAH!

GOD...I HATE THE WAY EVERYONE IN THE BAY AREA WORSHIPS NEW YORK! TRUST ME: IT'S HIGHLY OVER-RATED.

WELL...

LOOK... THERE'S NO WAY I'M MOVING TO NEW YORK FOR FOUR MONTHS, OKAY?

I KNOW.

I WASN'T REALLY ASKING YOU TO.

WELL, MAYBE SHE WANTS YOU TO TALK HER INTO STAYING.

YEAH, RIGHT. SHE DEFINITELY DOESN'T WANT THAT.

SHE THINKS IT'LL BE GOOD FOR US TO HAVE SOME "TIME OFF."

SO ARE YOU GUYS, LIKE, BROKEN UP?

33

WHAT DID I JUST SAY? WE'RE TAKING SOME TIME OFF.

OKAY, JEEZ...

WILL YOU STILL BE ABLE TO AFFORD YOUR PLACE?

YEAH...SHE ALREADY GAVE ME HER HALF OF FOUR MONTHS' RENT.

OH, RIGHT... THE TRUST FUND. SO WHEN DOES SHE LEAVE?

END OF THE MONTH. TCH...NOW I'M SUPPOSED TO BE ALL "SUPPORTIVE" AND HELP HER GET READY.

GOD...

SHE'LL BE GONE BEFORE I KNOW IT.

WELL, THIS HAS BEEN FUN...

I'M GONNA GO PAY THE BILL.

Hegenberger Rd.
Oakland Airport
⇩
EXIT ⇩ ONLY

THANKS FOR TAKING OFF WORK TONIGHT.

WHAT ELSE WAS I GONNA DO? MAKE YOU TAKE A SHUTTLE?

I THINK THINGS WILL BE PRETTY CRAZY WHEN I FIRST GET THERE, BUT I'LL GIVE YOU A CALL AFTER I GET SETTLED IN.

I'M REALLY GONNA MISS YOU.

TCH... IT'S ONLY A FEW MONTHS. YOU'RE GOING TO LOVE BEING A BACHELOR AGAIN.

YEAH, RIGHT.

COME ON... LET'S NOT GET ALL—

OH FUCK!

WHAT IS THIS? TRAFFIC AT EIGHT PM?

GOD DAMN IT!

HONK HONK

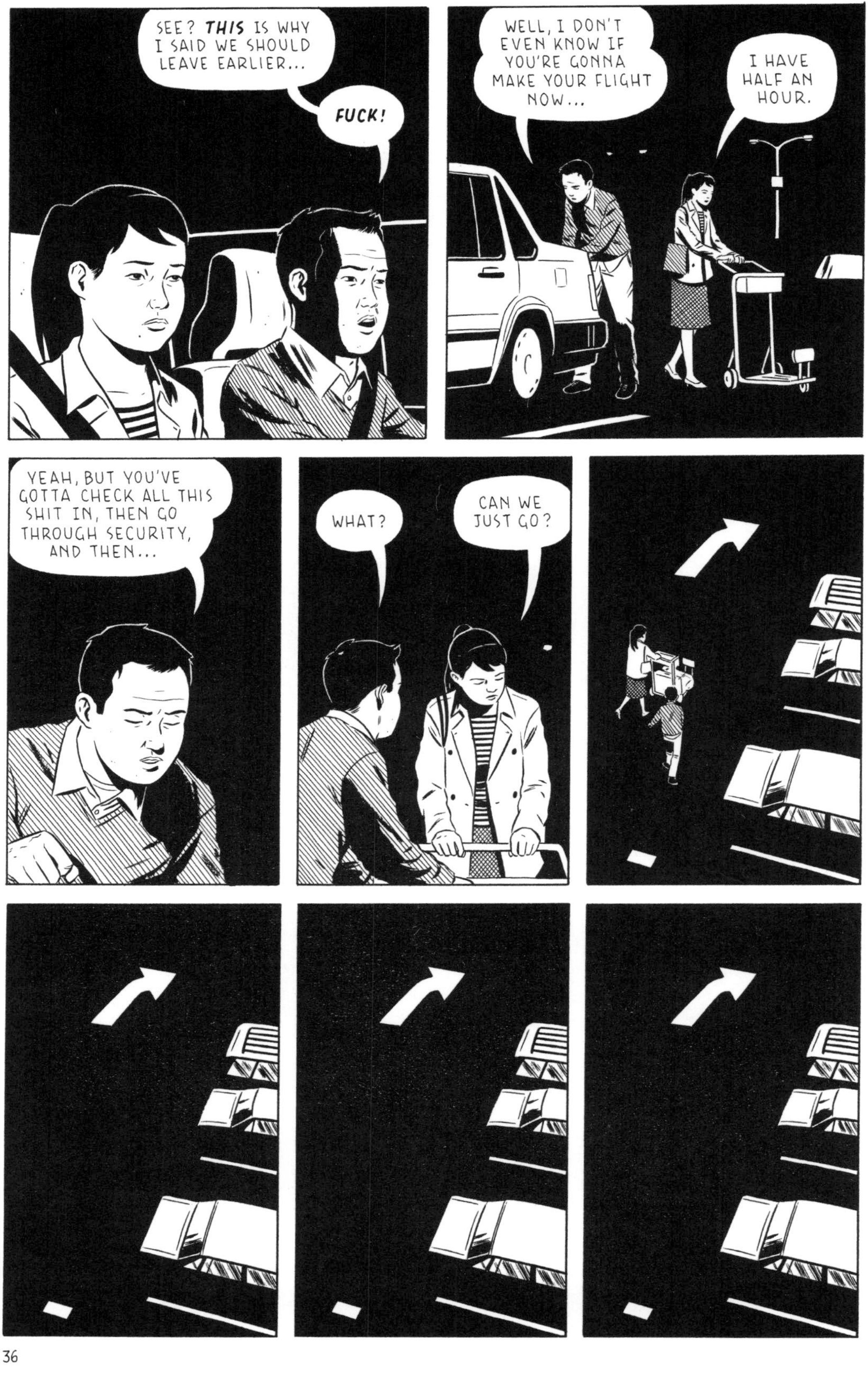
SEE? THIS IS WHY I SAID WE SHOULD LEAVE EARLIER...
FUCK!
WELL, I DON'T EVEN KNOW IF YOU'RE GONNA MAKE YOUR FLIGHT NOW...
I HAVE HALF AN HOUR.
YEAH, BUT YOU'VE GOTTA CHECK ALL THIS SHIT IN, THEN GO THROUGH SECURITY, AND THEN...
WHAT?
CAN WE JUST GO?

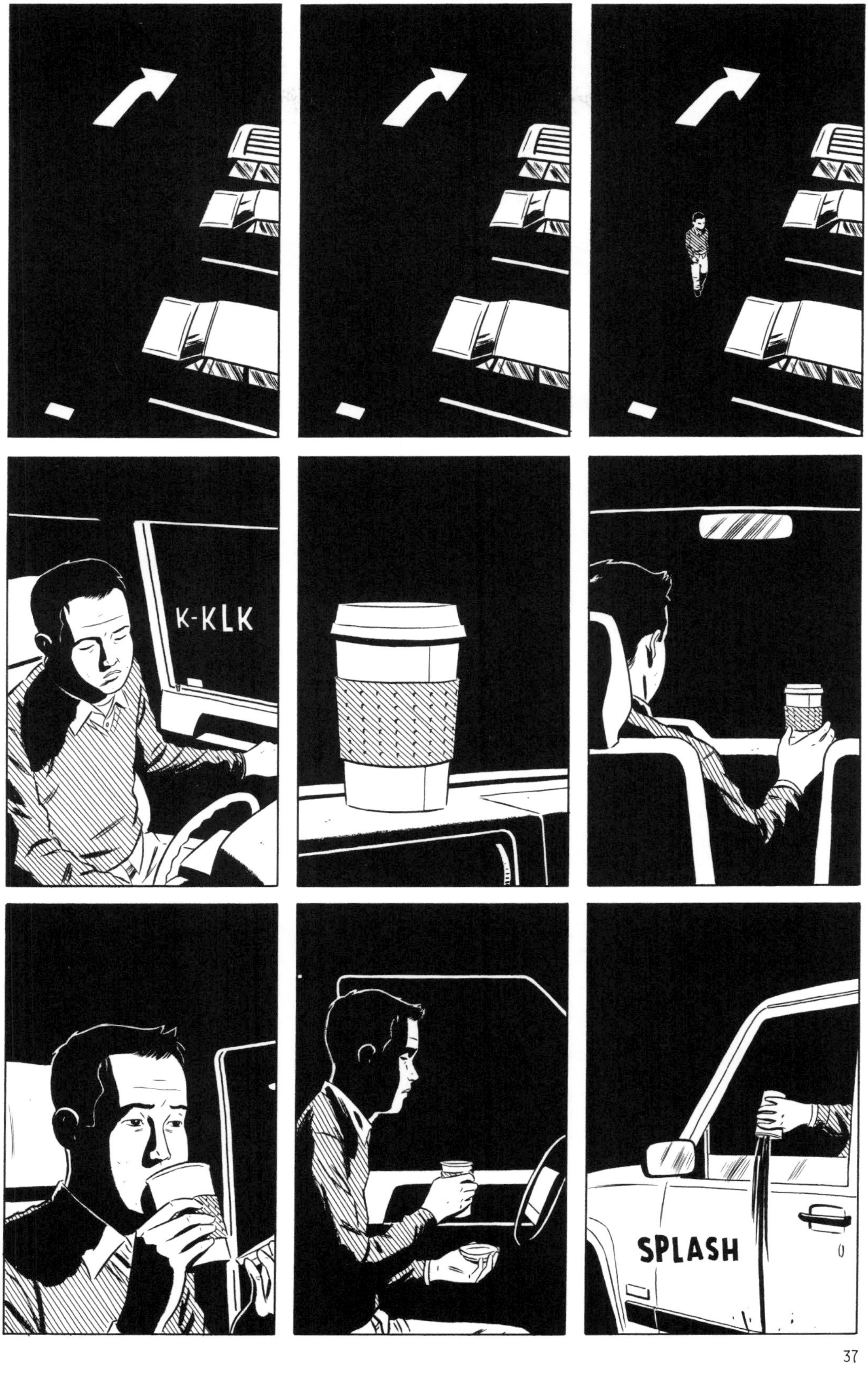
K-KLK
SPLASH

HEY, IT'S BEN.

YEAH, I JUST GOT BACK.

SO WHAT'S THE DEAL? ARE YOU STANDING ON A CHAIR WITH A NOOSE AROUND YOUR NECK?

NOT YET. I GUESS IT HASN'T REALLY HIT ME THAT SHE'S GONE.

OF **COURSE** I'M GONNA MISS HER. THAT'S NOT EVEN A...

YEAH...THE QUESTION IS WHETHER OR NOT SHE'LL MISS **ME**.

WELL, IF YOU WANT HER TO, THEN YOU'RE GONNA HAVE TO BE STRATEGIC. YOU CAN'T ACT ALL PATHETIC AND LONELY AND DESPERATE.

BUT THAT'S MY SPECIALTY! THAT'S WHAT I...

I KNOW. SHE MADE A POINT OF SAYING, BASICALLY, "DON'T CALL ME, I'LL CALL YOU."

NO, I THINK SHE JUST MEANT FOR THE FIRST FEW DAYS.

I KNOW.

WELL, LISTEN... ARE YOU DOING ANYTHING RIGHT NOW?

IF ALL GOES ACCORDING TO PLAN. YOU WON'T BELIEVE WHO'S OVER HERE RIGHT NOW!

HUH... WELL, GOOD LUCK.

YEAH, I GUESS YOU DON'T.

SKREEEE

Telephone
Address

RRING

RRING

RRING

CLICK
HELLO?

HI...

AUTUMN?

CHAPTER TWO

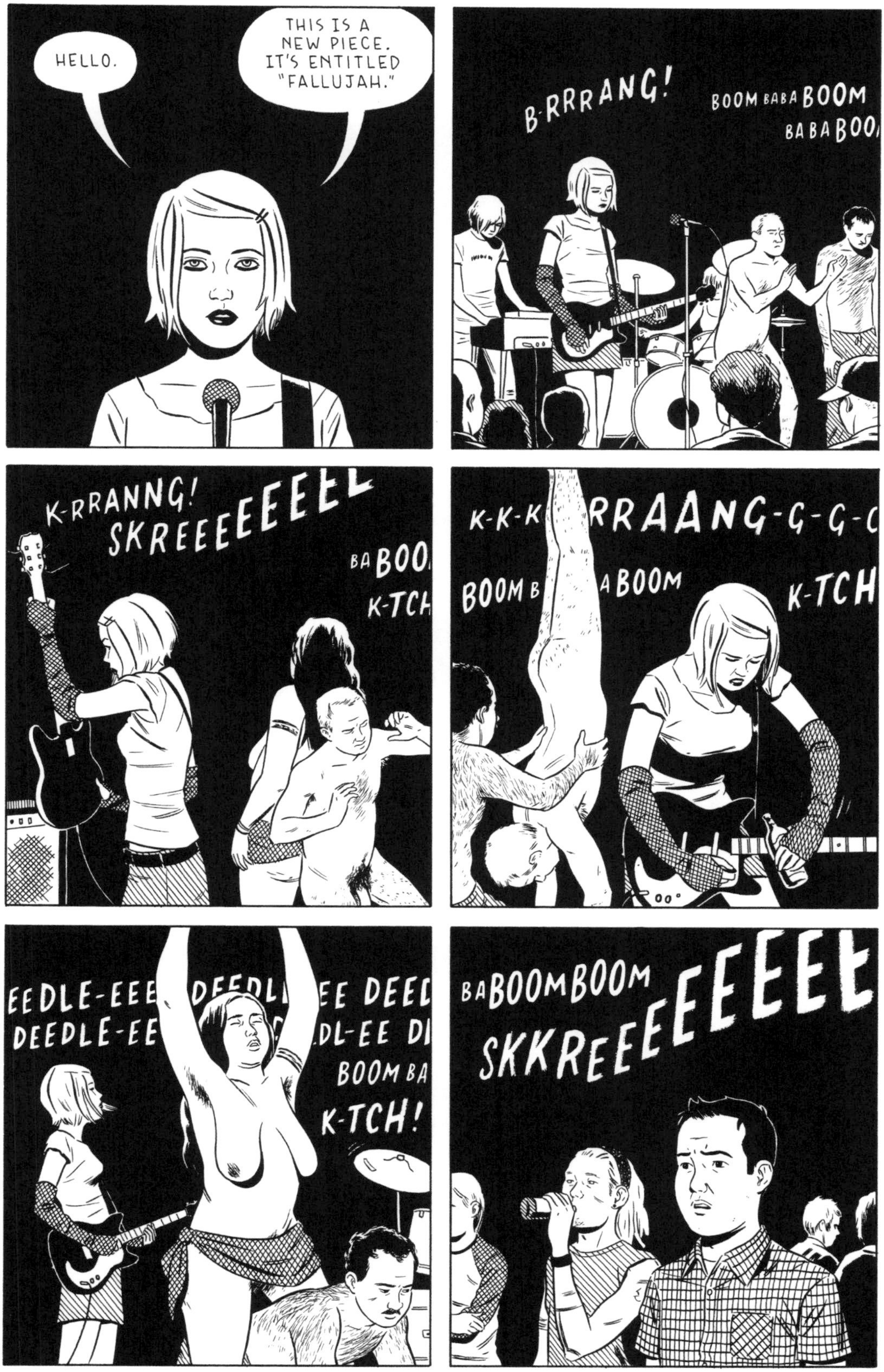
HELLO.
THIS IS A NEW PIECE. IT'S ENTITLED "FALLUJAH."
B-RRRANG!
BOOM BABA BOOM
BABA BOO
K-RRANNG!
SKREEEEEEEE
BA BOO
K-TCH
K-K-K RRAANG-G-G-G
BOOM B A BOOM
K-TCH
EEDLE-EEE DEEDL EE DEED
DEEDLE-EE DL-EE D
BOOM BA
K-TCH!
BA BOOM BOOM
SKREEEEEEEE

REALLY? GOD... THE WHOLE TIME I WAS UP THERE I WAS THINKING, "HE'S TOTALLY HATING THIS!"

NO! I WAS JUST... OVERWHELMED!

IT WAS LIKE A COMBINATION OF, OF... EXPERIMENTAL MUSIC, PERFORMANCE ART...

WELL, WE'RE TAKING THE PHYSICALITY OF MODERN DANCE AND THE IMPROVISATION OF FREE JAZZ AND INFUSING IT WITH A PUNK SENSIBILITY.

WOW. YEAH.

I HAVE TO ADMIT, I DIDN'T REALLY KNOW WHAT TO EXPECT, BUT THAT WAS...AMAZING.

THAT'S SO COOL!

SOMETHING WRONG WITH THE USUAL PLACE?

I'M KIND OF, UH... DODGING THAT WAITRESS.

WHY? I THOUGHT YOU WERE...

ENH...I HAD MY FILL.

SHE STARTED GETTING ALL *ATTACHED*.

HEAVEN FORBID...

SO, WHAT'S GOING ON WITH YOU AND MIKO?

WE'VE BEEN TALKING ON THE PHONE, BUT I'M NOT GONNA JUST SIT AROUND PINING AWAY FOR HER.

WHAT?

I THOUGHT YOU SAID YOU GUYS WEREN'T BROKEN UP.

WE'RE TAKING SOME TIME OFF. THOSE WERE *HER* WORDS.

SO I FIGURE, WHILE THE CAT IS AWAY, THE MOUSE WILL PLAY.

KNOWING YOU, THE "MOUSE" WILL JUST BE PLAYING WITH HIMSELF.

FUNNY.

WHAT IF I TOLD YOU I'VE ALREADY GONE OUT WITH AUTUMN TWICE?

THAT GIRL FROM THE THEATER? HELLO, MR. HUMBERT!

OH, COME ON...

SHE'S *TWENTY-TWO*, OKAY? THAT'S AT *LEAST* AS OLD AS YOUR LITTLE WAITRESS.

45

YEAH, BUT I'M A GIRL. IT'S DIFFERENT.

SO HOW FAR HAVE YOU GOTTEN?

UH, LET'S NOT GET INTO THIS.

I KNEW IT! LISTEN TO ME, BEN...

IF YOU HANG OUT WITH HER ONE MORE TIME AND DON'T MAKE A MOVE, BE PREPARED TO BE BANISHED TO "NEUTERED ASIAN FRIEND" TERRITORY FOREVER!

YOU MIGHT ALREADY BE ON YOUR WAY...

NEVER! I SHALL NEVER RETURN TO THAT HORRIBLE LAND AGAIN!

SO... HOW'S WORK?

WELL, THEY'RE DOING THOSE SEISMIC INSPECTIONS NOW, WHICH IS A HUGE HASSLE. THESE IDIOTS ACT LIKE THEY'RE FBI AGENTS OR SOMETHING, YOU KNOW?

AND IT'S LIKE, "YOU'RE LOOKING FOR CRACKS, OKAY?" IT'S A TOTAL NIGHTMARE.

YEAH, I BET.

SO HOW'S THE INTERN-SHIP GOING? YOU HAVEN'T TOLD ME MUCH ABOUT IT.

OH, I'VE LEARNED NOT TO BORE YOU.

BUT IT'S INCREDIBLE. I'M MEETING SO MANY AMAZING PEOPLE.

THAT'S GREAT.

I KEEP HAVING THESE MOMENTS WHERE I'LL STOP AND THINK, "WOW... I'M IN *NEW YORK CITY!*"

WELL, THAT *IS* WHERE YOU ARE...

I KNOW, BEN. YOU DON'T HAVE TO GET ALL SARCASTIC JUST BECAUSE I'M ENJOYING MYSELF.

WHAT? *YOU* STARTED IT WITH THAT "I'VE LEARNED NOT TO BORE YOU" COMMENT! I'M TRYING TO ACT INTERESTED, AND YOU...

"YOU STARTED IT"? HOW OLD ARE YOU? AND WHY CAN'T YOU EVER JUST BE *GENUINELY* INTERESTED?

YOU REALLY WANT ME TO ANSWER THAT?

YOU KNOW WHAT? MAYBE WE SHOULD JUST NOT TALK FOR AWHILE. THIS IS—

FINE.

SLAM!

I PROBABLY DIDN'T NEED THAT LAST DRINK.

HA HA YOU HAD TWO AMSTEL LIGHTS! THAT'S NOTHING COMPARED TO ME.

SORRY ABOUT THE MESS.

WOW... WHAT'S THIS?

OH, THAT'S ONE OF MY WORKS-IN-PROGRESS.

I WAKE UP EVERY MORNING, GO PEE, AND THEN TAKE A PICTURE. I'VE BEEN DOING IT SINCE JANUARY.

2/16/04

2/17/

ARE YOU SERIOUS?

WELL...YEAH. PATTERNS START TO EMERGE...LIKE WHEN I'M DEHYDRATED, OR WHEN I GET MY PERIOD...

IT'LL BE A HUGE INSTALLATION SOMEDAY.

THAT'S PRETTY AMAZING.

LET'S GO IN THE KITCHEN. I THINK MY ROOMMATE MIGHT BE SLEEPING.

OOH...WANT SOME CHAI? I'M TOTALLY CHAI-OBSESSED RIGHT NOW.

AUTUMN...

OH!

GOD, I'M SORRY, I...

WHAT ABOUT YOUR GIRL-FRIEND?

OH. I THOUGHT I TOLD YOU. WE'RE, UH... WE SPLIT UP. DON'T WORRY ABOUT THAT.

UM...

I'M JUST NOT REALLY INTO KISSING.

YOU KNOW... *GERMS*.

I SHOULD PROBABLY GET GOIN'

I'M SORRY, OKAY?

SO SHE'LL WRITHE AROUND ON STAGE WITH A BUNCH OF NAKED CREEPS, AND SHE'LL TAKE PHOTOS OF HER PISS EVERY DAY, BUT KISSING ME... APPARENTLY THAT'S *TOO DISGUSTING* FOR HER!

AH, IT'S FOR THE BEST. I MEAN, HOW COULD YOU EVEN GET IT UP FOR SOMEONE WHO DOES THAT KIND OF STUPID BULLSHIT?

WELL, IN THIS CASE, MY SUPERFICIALITY COULD'VE OVERPOWERED MY SNOBBERY.

OH, I FORGOT... SHE'S WHITE!

FUCK YOU.

YOU'RE JUST OUT OF PRACTICE. COME WITH ME TO THIS PARTY ON SATURDAY AND YOU CAN WATCH THE MASTER IN ACTION.

CAN I GIVE YOU MY TIME SHEETS?

OH, YEAH... GREAT. BUSY NIGHT, HUH?

MM... I GUESS.

AUTUMN... IS EVERYTHING OKAY?

OH.

SOMEONE SAID THE MEN'S ROOM WAS FLOODED AGAIN.

WELL...WISH ME LUCK TONIGHT.

LUCK? YOU'D PROBABLY BE BETTER OFF WITH A SEX-CHANGE!

WHAT? IS THIS A...YOU BROUGHT ME TO A *DYKE* PARTY?

SHHH! IT'S A MILLS PARTY, SO TECHNICALLY... NO.

BUT THE ODDS AREN'T IN YOUR FAVOR.

OH, CHEER UP. WOULD YOU RATHER BE GETTING BLUE-BALLED BY THE PEE GIRL AGAIN?

KNOCK KNOCK KNOCK

HEY! ALICE KIM!

HEY!

JESS, THIS IS MY FRIEND BEN.

ALL RIGHT, BEN! I HEARD ABOUT YOU, DUDE!

OH... HI.

YEAH, THERE'S DEFINITELY GONNA BE SOME WHITE CHICKS HERE TONIGHT, BEN! HA HA

THAT'S GREAT. THANK YOU.

LOOK WHO'S HERE!

RELAX.

HEY, A WHAT'S U

ALICE!

HOW GOIN

WHAT DO YOU WANT TO DRINK?

COME HERE! HAVE YOU MET CELESTE?

N'T ERE ING!

HELLO.

UH, HI...

IS THERE A BOTTLE OPENER...?

WHAT FOR? IT'S TWIST-OFF.

OH... IT IS?

UNNGGH!

HA HA HA HAHA AHAHA AHA

I'M JUST FUCKING WITH YOU.

YOU MUST BE ALICE'S FRIEND.

SUPPOSEDLY. UH...MY NAME'S BEN.

HI.

I'M SASHA. I'LL BET YOU WE HAVE SOMETHING IN COMMON.

YEAH? WHAT'S THAT?

WE'RE PROBABLY THE ONLY TWO PEOPLE AT THIS PARTY THAT ALICE KIM HASN'T SEDUCED.

REALLY? YOU'VE MANAGED TO...?

YEAH, I DODGED THAT BULLET. NO OFFENSE.

NO... NONE TAKEN.

APPARENTLY THAT'S QUITE AN ACCOMPLISHMENT AROUND HERE.

WHY'D YOU COME TO THIS THING? NOT TO MEET GIRLS, I HOPE.

YEAH, RIGHT.

IT'S LIKE, "WATER, WATER EVERYWHERE..."

ARE YOU THIRSTY?

UH...

NO...HA HA. I MEAN, I'M GONNA GO GET A BEER. DO YOU...?

OH, YEAH. THAT SOUNDS...

THERE YOU ARE!

SLAM!

LET'S GO.

HI SASHA.

I GUESS WE'RE LEAVING, BUT...I WORK AT THE UNIVERSITY THEATER. COME SEE A MOVIE FOR FREE SOMETIME.

OKAY.

AND POPCORN, TOO!

FREE POPCORN!

"FREE POPCORN"? HOW DO THE GIRLS RESIST YOU, BEN?

SHUT UP. WHY'D WE HAVE TO LEAVE ALL OF A SUDDEN?

I'M SICK OF THOSE DUMB BITCHES. AND LET ME TELL YOU ABOUT SASHA LENZ. SHE'S A *FENCE-SITTER*, OKAY? TOTAL BAD NEWS!

NO...THAT'S *GREAT* NEWS! ACTUALLY, IT'S PERFECT...

OH, GOD. DON'T EVEN START DOWN THIS ROAD.

IF I'M GONNA TRY TO... *BE* WITH A WHITE GIRL FOR THE FIRST TIME, MAYBE IT'S A GOOD THING IF SHE'S A LESBIAN!

SHE'S NOT A...I *TOLD YOU*, SHE'S A FENCE-SITTER! AND DO YOU EVEN REALIZE HOW *RETARDED* YOU SOUND?

YEAH, BUT STILL...

MAYBE SHE WON'T BE SO, UH...SIZE-CONSCIOUS.

OH MY FUCKING GOD. IS THAT REALLY HOW YOUR SICK MIND WORKS?

WHAT?

THAT'S JUST, LIKE, A BONUS. I ALREADY THOUGHT SHE WAS GREAT. I MEAN, SHE SEEMS SMART, FUNNY...

OH, RIGHT... YOUR TOP TWO CRITERIA.

GOD, YOU'RE FULL OF SHIT!

SMOKE PIT

SO ARE YOU REALLY ALL HUNG UP ON THOSE STEREOTYPES ABOUT... *SIZE*?

CAN WE TALK ABOUT SOMETHING ELSE?

COME ON. I'M CURIOUS.

LOOK... STEREOTYPES DON'T JUST MATERIALIZE OUT OF THIN AIR, OKAY?

HAVEN'T YOU EVER HEARD THAT STUPID JOKE?

UH..."WHAT'S THE MAIN DIFFERENCE BETWEEN ASIAN AND CAUCASIAN MEN?"

I WOULDN'T KNOW.

"THE CAUC."

EW!

I ACTUALLY HEARD A GIRL TELL THAT JOKE IN COLLEGE! I WAS STANDING RIGHT THERE AND SHE—

OKAY, OKAY...

HOW SMALL ARE WE TALKING HERE? LIKE, IN INCHES?

YEAH...LIKE I'M GONNA GIVE YOU AN ACTUAL MEASUREMENT...

ARE WE TALKING LESS THAN FIVE INCHES? FOUR?

FORGET IT.

OH MY GOD. IS IT *THREE*?

END OF CONVERSATION.

YOUR REFUSAL TO ANSWER ONLY DAMNS YOU FURTHER, BEN!

MM-HMM?

SO, WE'VE GOT ANOTHER SHOW COMING UP THIS WEEKEND.

OH YEAH? THAT'S GREAT.

I CAN GET YOU ON THE LIST, IF YOU WANT.

UH...WHAT NIGHT IS IT? BECAUSE I MIGHT HAVE TO—

TAP
TAP
TAP

HI.

REMEMBER ME?

I LOVE THIS PLACE. I DON'T THINK THERE'S A SINGLE HEALTHY ITEM ON THE MENU.

I KNOW. MY EX WOULD NEVER EAT HERE FOR THAT EXACT REASON.

HEY! IT'S ANOTHER THING WE HAVE IN COMMON: OVERLY HEALTH-CONSCIOUS EX-GIRLFRIENDS.

SORRY. WE DON'T NEED TO TALK ABOUT—

NO, NO... IT'S INTERESTING. WHAT'S HER NAME? WHAT'S SHE LIKE?

HER NAME'S MIKO AND, UH, SHE'S JAPANESE, SO... YOU KNOW...

WHAT DOES *THAT* MEAN? THAT THEY ALL LOOK ALIKE?

NO, I JUST MEAN... YOU KNOW: BLACK HAIR, BROWN EYES, ETC., ETC.

WHAT ABOUT *YOUR* EX? WHAT'S SHE LIKE?

CAITLIN? OH... SHE'S A DYKE.

REALLY? LIKE, WITH THE LITTLE RAT-TAIL AND THE FANNY-PACK...?

WHAT?

HARDLY. SHE LOOKS LIKE A VERY STYLISH, HANDSOME BOY. SHE'S QUITE STUNNING, REALLY.

I DON'T GET THAT. I MEAN, IF YOU'RE INTO GIRLS, WOULDN'T YOU WANT TO BE WITH A...

BEN, DO YOU REALLY THINK YOU CAN BE SO LOGICAL ABOUT WHAT TURNS YOUR HEAD?

OH, I SHOULD SHUT UP. I'M SURE IT'S *FASCINATING* TO HEAR ME GO ON AND ON ABOUT GRAD SCHOOL POLITICS.

ZZZZZ

GOD... I'M SORRY! I ALWAYS DO THIS.

I'M JUST KIDDING. IT ACTUALLY MAKES ME FEEL A LITTLE BETTER ABOUT DROPPING OUT.

YEAH... IT'S SUCH A WEIRD FEELING TALK-ING TO SOMEONE WHO ISN'T TOTALLY IMMERSED IN ACADEMIA.

THANK YOU.

NO, IT'S GOOD FOR ME. SOMETIMES IT FEELS LIKE I'M HERMETICALLY SEALED IN THAT WORLD, AND IT'S JUST... TIRESOME.

WELL, YOU'RE ALMOST DONE, RIGHT?

YEAH, AND THEN I CAN GET A JOB DOING RESEARCH, WHICH IS BASICALLY THE SAME THING...

WELL, I THINK IT'S PRETTY ADMIRABLE.

I MEAN, MAYBE NOT AS ADMIRABLE AS MANAGING A CRAPPY MOVIE THEATER, BUT...

I LIKE TALKING TO YOU.

OH MY *GOD*... YOU HAVE THE SOFTEST SKIN I'VE EVER FELT!

ARE YOU A JUNKIE?

WHAT?

QUIT SNOOPING IN THERE!

WHAT IS THIS THING? "AUTO...INJECTOR"...?

OH...IT'S AN EPI-PEN.

A *WHAT*?

IT'S AN EMERGENCY SHOT FOR MY ALLERGIES.

DO YOU ALWAYS NOSE AROUND IN PEOPLE'S BATHROOMS?

MM...USUALLY, YEAH. WHAT ARE YOU ALLERGIC TO?

LET'S SEE...UH, PEANUTS, WALNUTS, ALMONDS, MACADAMIA NUTS, PINE NUTS, HAZELNUTS, CASHEWS...

...CRAB, LOBSTER, SHRIMP, SQUID, OCTOPUS, MILK, MILK PRODUCTS...

...BEE STINGS, OLIVE TREE BARK...

OLIVE TREE BARK?

YEAH, BUT NOT OLIVES, STRANGELY. I GUESS THAT'S ALL. THE NUTS ARE THE ONLY THINGS THAT ARE, LIKE, *FATAL*.

SO YOU'VE NEVER HAD A PEANUT BUTTER AND JELLY SANDWICH?

I KNOW, I KNOW... BIG TRAGEDY, RIGHT? I HEAR THIS ALL THE TIME.

ACTUALLY, YOU'RE NOT MISSING OUT ON MUCH.

I'VE ALWAYS HATED PEANUT BUTTER.

DO YOU THINK WE SHOULD, UH... I MEAN, CAN I GIVE YOU A KISS...?

OKAY... I'M GONNA PRETEND THAT YOU DIDN'T JUST DO THAT.

JESUS, WHAT'S *WRONG* WITH ME?

I'M SORRY... I DON'T KNOW WHAT I WAS—

NO...

I JUST MEANT... DON'T ASK FOR PERMISSION.

OKAY.

YOU'RE A GOOD KISSER.

I KNOW. I'M VERY ORALLY FIXATED.

LUCKY FOR YOUR GIRL-FRIENDS.

I'VE HAD BOYFRIENDS, TOO. I'M SURPRISED ALICE DIDN'T BRIEF YOU.

SHE MIGHT'VE ALLUDED TO SOMETHING, BUT...

BEN.

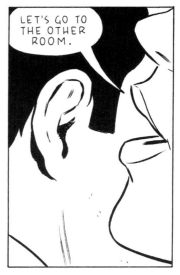

LET'S GO TO THE OTHER ROOM.

ARE YOU OKAY? I THINK YOU'RE ACTUALLY SHAKING.

IT'S JUST... THIS IS THE FIRST TIME I'VE EVER BEEN WITH...

WITH...?

I MEAN... IT'S, UH, BEEN AWHILE SINCE...

SHHH

I KNOW WHAT YOU WERE GOING TO SAY. THIS'LL BE A FIRST FOR ME, TOO.

WHAT? I THOUGHT YOU SAID—

SHHHH

THE EAGLE HAS LANDED.

WHAT...? *EW*, YOU SCORED WITH THE FENCE-SITTER?

I TOLD YOU TO STAY AWAY FROM HER!

OH MY GOD. YOU'RE ACTUALLY JEALOUS OF *ME* FOR ONCE!

OH, PLEASE.

DO YOU REALLY THINK I GIVE A SHIT ABOUT SOME TRENDY *DABBLER*? I COULD CARE LESS!

JESUS! CAN I JUST BASK IN MY GLORY FOR ONE FUCKING MINUTE?

SORRY... I'M IN A SHITTY MOOD.

APPARENTLY. AND I WAS GONNA REGALE YOU WITH DETAILS, TOO.

I KNOW. I JUST... I GOT KICKED OUT OF SCHOOL.

WHAT ARE YOU TALKING ABOUT?

JUST COME OVER AFTER WORK, OKAY?

AND BRING SOME BEER.

REMEMBER WHEN I TOOK YOU TO THAT STUPID PARTY?

AH, YES... THE FATEFUL NIGHT.

YEAH, WELL...I GOT INTO AN ARGUMENT WITH THIS *ANNOYING BITCH* THERE, AND—

ABOUT WHAT?

OH...I GUESS SHE'S THE ROOMMATE OF THAT WAITRESS FROM THE CREPE PLACE, AND... IT DOESN'T MATTER.

ANYWAY, I SAW HER ON CAMPUS THE OTHER DAY, AND IT... ESCALATED.

UH-OH. WHAT DOES *THAT* MEAN?

SHE STARTED TALKING SHIT AGAIN, SO I KICKED HER IN THE PUSSY.

JESUS! WHAT'S WRONG WITH YOU?

I WARNED HER! SHE COULD'VE JUST SHUT UP AND GOTTEN OUT OF MY FACE...

KLAK

SHE WENT AND REPORTED ME, SO NOW I'M TEMPORARILY SUSPENDED AND BANNED FROM THE CAMPUS.

SO YOU'RE NOT REALLY EXPELLED.

FUCK IT. I'M QUITTING.

WHAT ARE YOU TALKING ABOUT?

I'M GOING TO NEW YORK FOR A WHILE. I'VE GOT A COUPLE FRIENDS I CAN STAY WITH IN BROOKLYN. I NEED TO JUST...CLEAR MY HEAD.

YOU TOO? DOES EVERYONE IN BERKELEY HAVE A TOTAL *HARD-ON* FOR NEW YORK?

WHY DOESN'T THE ENTIRE BAY AREA JUST PACK UP AND MOVE TO NEW YORK AND GET IT OVER WITH?

WELL, WHY DON'T YOU COME WITH ME?

YEAH, RIGHT.

ARE YOU KIDDING ME? MY WHOLE LIFE IS HERE!

WHAT LIFE?

FUCK YOU. YOU'RE NOT REALLY GOING. YOU'RE JUST RILED UP RIGHT NOW.

I ALREADY BOOKED MY FLIGHT. I LEAVE ON TUESDAY.

JAPANESE SNAX

VIETNAM HOUSE

BEAR'S NOODLES

KOREAN BBQ

JESUS... WHAT IS THIS? AN ASIAN "GANGSTA" CONVENTION?

THEY'RE JUST COLLEGE KIDS, BEN.

DID YOU SEE THAT GUY? THE WAY HE LOOKED AT US?

WHO?

THAT GUY THAT JUST PASSED US. HE HAD WHITE-GIRL ENVY.

YOU'RE CRAZY.

NOW, IF *HE* HAD BEEN WITH A WHITE GIRL, TOO, WE WOULD'VE GIVEN EACH OTHER THE SIGN.

WHAT ARE YOU TALKING ABOUT?

IT'S A LITTLE CODE... A HAND SIGNAL WE GIVE EACH OTHER.

IT'S KIND OF LIKE A COVERT "HIGH FIVE."

OH MY GOD... PLEASE TELL ME YOU'RE JOKING.

YEAH, I JUST MADE THAT UP. I WAS JUST...

NEVER MIND. SORRY.

KNOCK KNOCK

HEY! I THOUGHT YOU WERE AT SCHOOL TODAY.

I HAD AN IMPULSIVE URGE TO SEE YOU.

ALSO, MY CLASS WAS CANCELLED.

LUCKY ME.

THUD

UM...

I THOUGHT MAYBE WE COULD... GET LUNCH OR SOMETHING.

OH... YEAH.

SORRY ABOUT THAT.

SO, THE NEWS IS NOT GOOD.

THE INSPECTORS HAVE FOUND SOME SERIOUS FLAWS IN THE STRUCTURE, AND IT LOOKS LIKE WE'LL HAVE TO SHUT DOWN FOR SEISMIC REPAIRS.

FOR HOW LONG?

WE DON'T KNOW YET.

PROBABLY A FEW MONTHS, AT LEAST. IF ANYONE'S INTERESTED IN TRANS-FERRING TO ANOTHER THEATER, LET ME KNOW. THERE MAY BE SOME OPENINGS IN THE CITY.

I'M SORRY, GUYS.

I NEED TO TALK TO YOU.

WHENEVER SOMEONE SAYS THAT, IT MEANS "I'M ABOUT TO REALLY BUM YOU OUT."

BEN, I LIKE YOU A LOT, AND I FEEL LIKE I NEED TO BE HONEST WITH YOU. ABOUT CAITLIN.

WHAT ABOUT HER?

WELL, SHE'S BEEN ON TOUR FOR THE PAST FEW MONTHS, AND I DIDN'T REALLY KNOW WHERE WE STOOD WHEN SHE LEFT.

AND NOW SHE'S BACK.

YEAH.

SO I'M GUESSING THIS ISN'T GOOD NEWS FOR ME.

IT'S MY FAULT. I'M SORRY.

HUH...IT JUST SEEMS KIND OF DECEPTIVE. I MEAN, YOU MADE IT PRETTY CLEAR THAT YOU TWO HAD BROKEN UP. I WOULDN'T HAVE PURSUED ANYTHING IF...

I KNOW.

IT'S A PROBLEM OF MINE. I'M NOT VERY GOOD AT BEING ALONE.

OH, REALLY?

THAT'S STRANGE, BECAUSE I *LOVE* BEING ALONE! IN FACT...

BEN... COME ON.

WELL, THAT'S GREAT. HAVE FUN BACK ON THE OTHER SIDE OF THE FENCE, OKAY?

JESUS CHRIST...

EVERY TIME I BREAK UP WITH SOMEONE, THEY PULL THIS SAME BULLSHIT. THIS DOESN'T HAVE ANY-THING TO DO WITH WHO *I* AM, OKAY? AND TO TELL YOU THE TRUTH, IT HAS NOTHING TO DO WITH CAITLIN, EITHER.

WELL, THIS SEEMS TO BE A LITTLE PROBLEM OF YOURS, HUH? TELLING THE TRUTH? YOU MIGHT WANT TO WORK ON—

LISTEN TO ME.

I COULD BE TOTALLY, BRUTALLY HONEST ABOUT WHY I'M DOING THIS, BUT I'M GOING TO RESTRAIN MYSELF BECAUSE I'M NOT SURE YOU'D EVER RECOVER.

CLOSED FOR RENOVATION

WE'LL BE BACK

Sapphic SORORITY

rRING

rRING

MOSHI-MOSHI! THIS IS MIKO... LEAVE ME A MESSAGE.

BEEP!

IT'S ME AGAIN.

I DON'T KNOW IF THERE'S A PROBLEM WITH YOUR VOICE-MAIL OR SOMETHING, BUT...UHH...

LOOK, IF YOU'RE NOT TOO BUSY RUNNING AROUND NEW YORK, I'D APPRECIATE IT IF YOU COULD JUST RETURN MY FUCKING CALLS.

OKAY?

'CAUSE THIS IS JUST... BULLSHIT.

SLAM!

UH, NEW YORK CITY. A LISTING FOR THE, UH, ASIAN-AMERICAN FILM INSTITUTE? MAYBE IT'S THE...INSTITUTE FOR INDEPENDENT ASIAN-AMERICAN CINEMA...?

NO, I'M NOT SURE.

CAN YOU... OKAY. YEAH. *THANKS.* YOU'VE BEEN *VERY* HELPFUL.

SLAM!
SLAM!
SLAM!

rRING

HELLO?

HEY!
IT'S ALICE!

OH.

HEY.

JEEZ...
NICE TO HEAR
FROM YOU, TOO,
ASSHOLE!

SORRY.
I WAS
JUST...

WHAT'S
UP?

LISTEN...YOU GOTTA COME TO
NEW YORK. YOU'RE OBVIOUSLY
ABOUT TO KILL YOURSELF IN
THAT APARTMENT, AND THERE'S
SOMETHING HERE THAT YOU
HAVE TO SEE WITH YOUR
OWN TWO EYES.

CHAPTER THREE

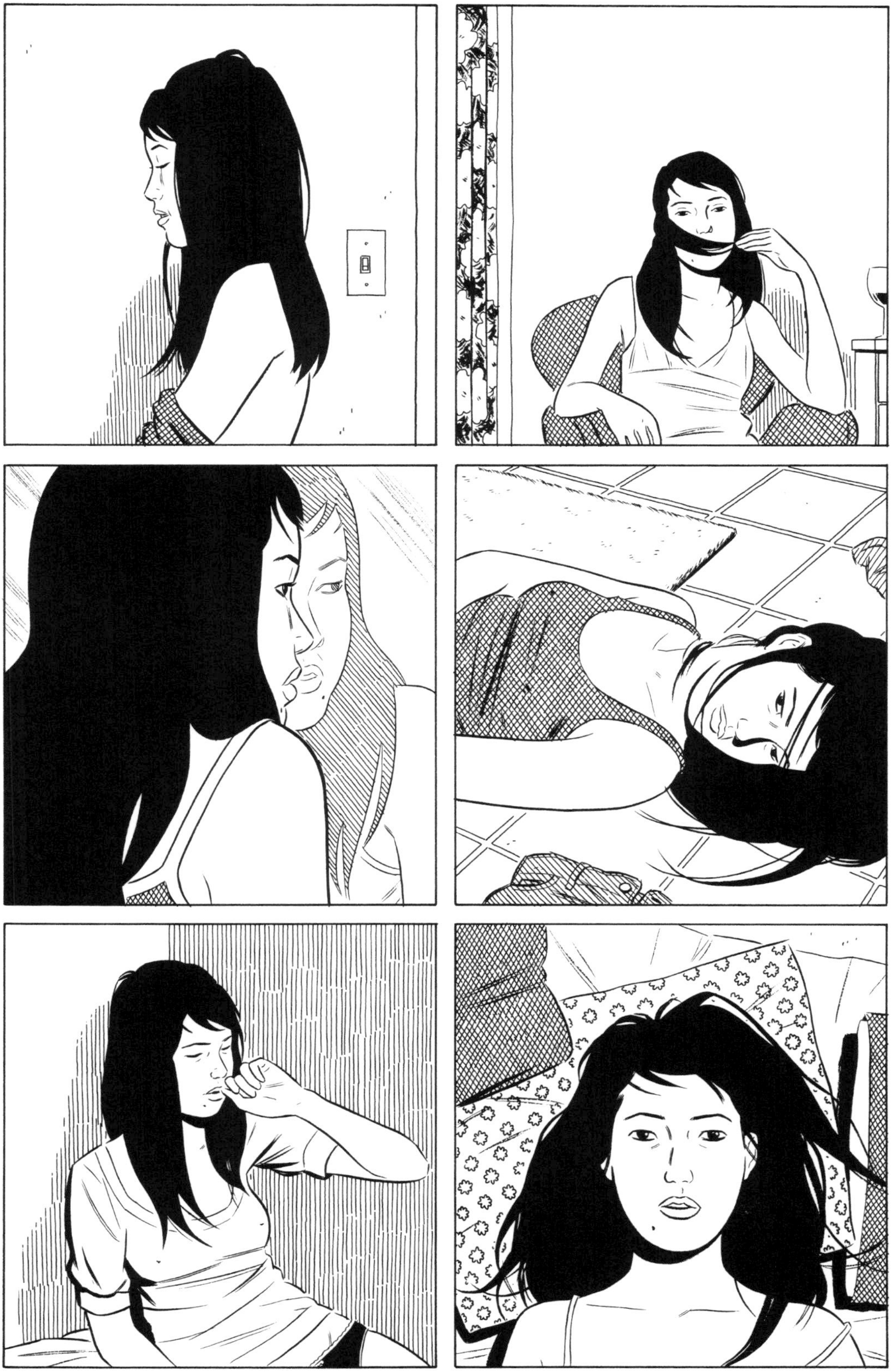

SO, WHAT DO YOU THINK? DID I DRAG YOU OUT HERE FOR NOTHING?

I MEAN, I KNOW ALL ASIAN GIRLS LOOK ALIKE TO YOU, BUT...

WILL YOU SHUT UP FOR A MINUTE WHILE I TRY TO... PROCESS THIS?

I'M CURIOUS ABOUT THE PHOTOS IN THE WINDOW...?

AREN'T THEY AMAZING?

DO YOU KNOW ANYTHING ABOUT THEM? WHERE THEY CAME FROM?

OH, LEON TAKES ALL THE PHOTOS HIMSELF.

AND LEON IS...?

LEON CHRISTOPHER. HE DESIGNS THE CLOTHES. THIS IS HIS SHOP.

AH... HUMILITY!

HEH HEH... IF YOU LIKE THE PHOTOS, YOU SHOULD TAKE ONE OF OUR POSTCARDS.

WHAT ABOUT THE GIRL IN THE PICTURES?

OH...

I HAVE NO IDEA WHERE HE FINDS THEM.

...AND RIGHT OVER THERE IS THE BROOKLYN BRIDGE.

DOESN'T IT MAKE YOU FEEL LIKE YOU'RE IN SOME NOSTALGIC MOVIE ABOUT BEING JEWISH OR SOMETHING?

MM-HMM.

LOOK...WE'RE STILL NOT A HUNDRED PERCENT SURE IT'S HER, RIGHT?

I THINK I'D RECOGNIZE MY OWN GIRLFRIEND, OKAY? IT JUST...DOESN'T MAKE SENSE.

YOUR "GIRLFRIEND"?

HOW MANY TIMES DO I HAVE TO TELL YOU? WE'RE *TAKING A —*

OKAY, OKAY!

DOES SHE KNOW YOU'RE HERE?

YEAH, RIGHT... BECAUSE I ALWAYS LIKE TO GIVE PEOPLE ADVANCE WARNING BEFORE I FLY ACROSS THE COUNTRY TO SPY ON THEM.

WE HAVEN'T TALKED IN, LIKE, TWO WEEKS. I FELT LIKE SHE WAS AVOIDING MY CALLS, SO I LEFT THIS, UH, *EMPHATIC* MESSAGE, AND NOW...

THE OLD "SELF-FULFILLING PROPHECY" VOICEMAIL.

YEAH.

K-CLIK

OH...!

I'M HOME!

HEY!

THIS MUST BE THE INFAMOUS BEN TANAKA!

SAY HELLO TO MEREDITH, OUR GRACIOUS HOSTESS.

GREAT TO MEET YOU.

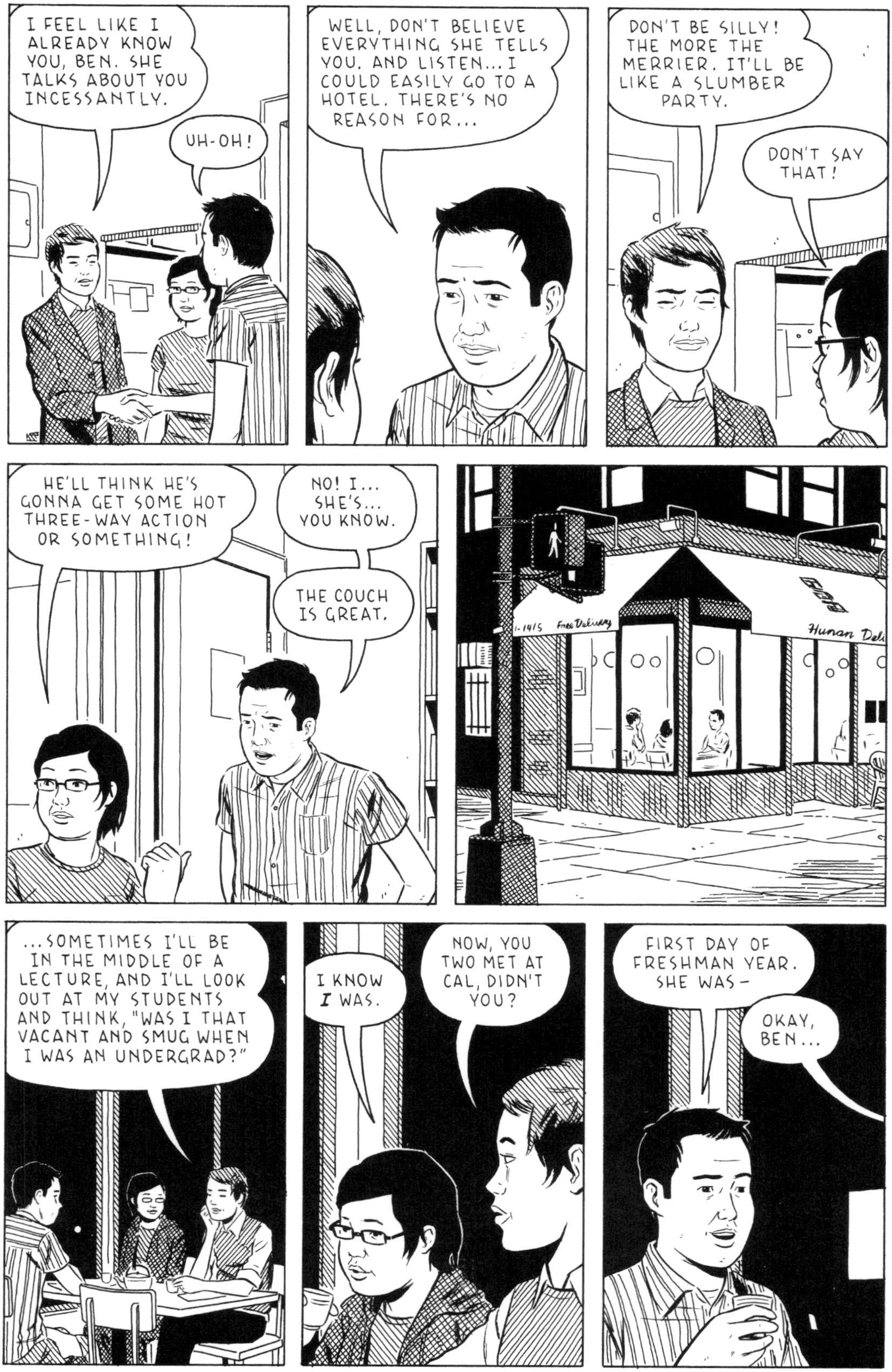
I FEEL LIKE I ALREADY KNOW YOU, BEN. SHE TALKS ABOUT YOU INCESSANTLY.
UH-OH!
WELL, DON'T BELIEVE EVERYTHING SHE TELLS YOU. AND LISTEN... I COULD EASILY GO TO A HOTEL. THERE'S NO REASON FOR...
DON'T BE SILLY! THE MORE THE MERRIER. IT'LL BE LIKE A SLUMBER PARTY.
DON'T SAY THAT!
HE'LL THINK HE'S GONNA GET SOME HOT THREE-WAY ACTION OR SOMETHING!
NO! I... SHE'S... YOU KNOW.
THE COUCH IS GREAT.
Free Delivery
Hunan Deli
...SOMETIMES I'LL BE IN THE MIDDLE OF A LECTURE, AND I'LL LOOK OUT AT MY STUDENTS AND THINK, "WAS I THAT VACANT AND SMUG WHEN I WAS AN UNDERGRAD?"
I KNOW *I* WAS.
NOW, YOU TWO MET AT CAL, DIDN'T YOU?
FIRST DAY OF FRESHMAN YEAR. SHE WAS—
OKAY, BEN...

I DON'T THINK WE NEED TO HEAR THIS BORING ANECDOTE.

I THINK WE DO! GO AHEAD, BEN.

SHE WAS IN THE DORM ROOM NEXT TO MINE, SO I WENT OVER TO INTRODUCE MYSELF, AND THERE SHE WAS, IN ALL HER PUNKY, DYKEY GLORY, HAMMERING A GIANT "SILENCE = DEATH" FLAG ONTO THE WALL.

SO WE MADE OUR INTRODUCTIONS, AND THEN... I DON'T KNOW WHY, BUT I POINTED AT THE FLAG AND SAID, "UH... SO YOU'RE GAY?"

TCH!

YEAH... WHAT KIND OF IDIOT SAYS THAT?

WELL, BUT WHAT KIND OF IDIOT GLARES BACK AT ME AND SAYS, "I DON'T THINK THAT'S ANY OF YOUR BUSINESS"?

PFFF HAHA

ALL RIGHT. SO I WAS "FINDING MYSELF."

SCREW YOU.

I THINK IT'S ADORABLE.

SO, WERE YOU GUYS FRIENDS AT MILLS? IS THAT HOW...?

OH, WE KNEW EACH OTHER TANGENTIALLY WHEN I WAS OUT THERE, BUT WE CERTAINLY WEREN'T *FRIENDS*.

WHAT WOULD YOU SAY?

RIVALS?

WE MIGHT'VE PURSUED A FEW OF THE SAME LADIES, BUT...

SHE WAS A WORTHY COMPETITOR. WE EVEN GOT INTO A FEW TIFFS, IF I REMEMBER CORRECTLY.

DID SHE EVER THREATEN TO KICK YOU IN THE PUSSY?

UH...

I THINK I'D REMEMBER IF SHE DID, BUT...

I'M SORRY. JUST IGNORE HIM.

NO, NO... THAT'S NOT *MY* PHRASE! IT'S SOMETHING THAT SHE—

LET IT GO, BEN.

LET'S, UH...LET'S FIGURE OUT WHAT WE'RE ORDERING.

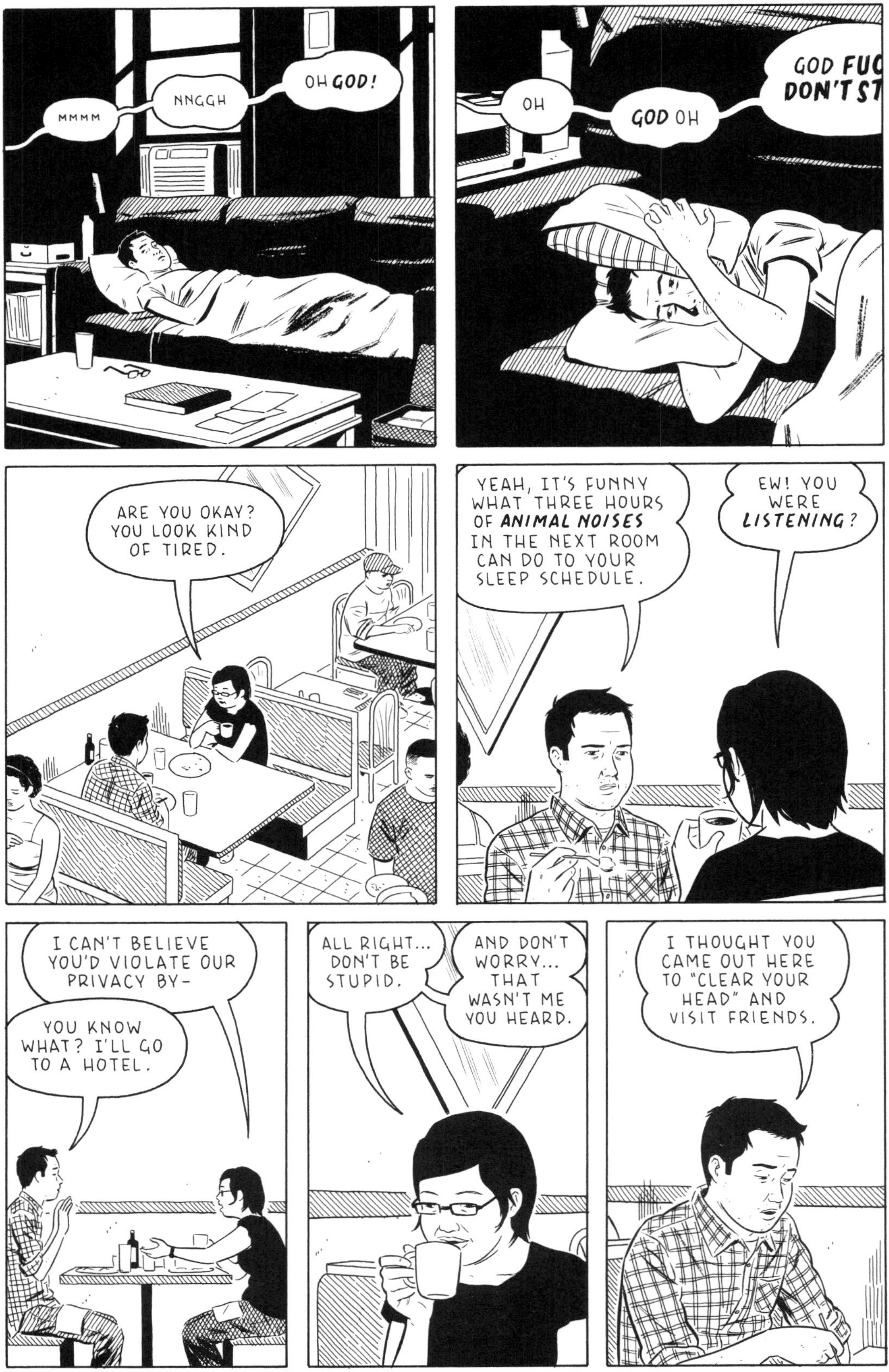
MMMM
NNGGH
OH GOD!
OH
GOD OH
GOD FUC
DON'T ST
ARE YOU OKAY? YOU LOOK KIND OF TIRED.
YEAH, IT'S FUNNY WHAT THREE HOURS OF ANIMAL NOISES IN THE NEXT ROOM CAN DO TO YOUR SLEEP SCHEDULE.
EW! YOU WERE LISTENING?
I CAN'T BELIEVE YOU'D VIOLATE OUR PRIVACY BY-
YOU KNOW WHAT? I'LL GO TO A HOTEL.
ALL RIGHT... DON'T BE STUPID.
AND DON'T WORRY... THAT WASN'T ME YOU HEARD.
I THOUGHT YOU CAME OUT HERE TO "CLEAR YOUR HEAD" AND VISIT FRIENDS.

WELL, THOSE FRIENDS TOOK ME TO A PARTY WHERE I RAN INTO MEREDITH, AND PLANS CHANGED.

SHE OFFERED TO LET ME CRASH ON HER COUCH, WHICH I DID FOR ONE NIGHT, AND THEN... I WAS SUMMONED TO THE BEDROOM.

JESUS.

WELL, SHE SEEMS REALLY NICE.

"REALLY NICE"? FUCK YOU! SHE'S LIKE MY TOTAL DREAM GIRL!

SO YOU'RE STILL IN *THAT* PHASE, HUH?

LOOK...I'D LIKE TO AT LEAST *TRY* TO NOT FUCK THIS ONE UP, OKAY? SO MAYBE YOU CAN HOLD OFF ON THE PUSSY-KICKING ANECDOTES?

YOU'RE MORE FUN IN CALIFORNIA.

SO WHAT ARE YOU GONNA DO ABOUT MIKO? IS IT OVER, OR...?

HUH? WHY WOULD IT BE OVER?

Free

WELL, WHAT ABOUT THOSE SKANKY PHOTOS? IT'S LIKE SHE'S BEEN LIVING SOME SECRET EXHIBITIONIST LIFE OUT HERE.

SO SHE WANTED TO TRY MODELING OR WHATEVER.

SHE PROBABLY THOUGHT I'D BE DISCOURAGING OR CRITICAL IF SHE TOLD ME ABOUT IT.

AND SHE'D BE WRONG?

NO...THAT'S THE POINT! I WOULD'VE BEEN A *TOTAL PRICK* ABOUT IT.

LOOK...IT'S EMBARR-ASSING AND KIND OF PATHETIC FOR HER TO WANT TO DO THAT, BUT, YOU KNOW... I ACTED LIKE I *LOVED* THE PEE GIRL'S RIDICULOUS "ART."

AND I SAT THERE AND LISTENED INTENTLY WHILE THE FENCE-SITTER DRONED ON AND ON ABOUT GRAD SCHOOL BULLSHIT.

SO I HAVE TO BE SUPPORTIVE OF SOME STUPID SHIT. BIG DEAL.

YEAH, BUT AT LEAST YOU WERE HORNY FOR THOSE OTHER GIRLS, SO THAT MADE IT EASIER.

JESUS... I NEVER SAID I *WASN'T* ATTRACTED TO MIKO, OKAY?

I WAS JUST... IDEALIZING WHAT I COULDN'T HAVE, YOU KNOW? IT HAPPENS.

MM-HMN.

YOU SHOULD KNOW. IT STARTS HAPPENING TO *YOU* AFTER THE SECOND OR THIRD DATE!

SO NOW YOU'VE GOTTEN THE WHOLE "WHITE PRIZE" THING OUT OF YOUR SYSTEM, AND YOU'RE READY TO GO BACK TO YOUR NICE JAPANESE GIRLFRIEND.

IT HAS NOTHING TO DO WITH... *JESUS CHRIST!* WHO ARE YOU... ELVIN WANG?

ASIAN-AMERICAN INDEPENDENT FILM INSTITUTE

I'M SORRY. WHAT WAS THE LAST NAME AGAIN?

HAYASHI. SHE'S AN INTERN HERE.

HM. WELL ACTUALLY, *I'M* THE ONLY INTERN HERE RIGHT NOW. BUT I JUST STARTED A FEW WEEKS AGO, SO...

CAN YOU CHECK TO SEE IF MAYBE SHE WORKED HERE BEFORE YOU, OR...?

I'M AFRAID WE CAN'T GIVE OUT THAT KIND OF INFORMATION.

SORRY.

WELL, SO MUCH FOR MY BIG ROMANTIC SURPRISE.

FUCKING LYING BITCH.

HEY, WATCH IT!

OOPS... JUST KIDDING.

SO NOW WHAT?

HOW DO WE GET TO GREENE STREET?

GOD... I CAN'T BELIEVE SHE CAN AFFORD A PLACE AROUND HERE.

I'D GIVE ANY-THING TO HAVE RICH PARENTS THAT DIED IN A PLANE CRASH.

CAR CRASH. CAN YOU SEE THE DOOR?

RELAX. I'VE GOT IT ALL STAKED OUT.

SO LISTEN... I'M THINKING ABOUT MAYBE NOT GOING BACK TO SCHOOL.

REALLY? WHAT ABOUT THE Ph.D.?

MAYBE IT'LL JUST BE A TEMPORARY BREAK. BUT WHEN I'M REALLY HONEST WITH MYSELF, THERE'S ONLY ONE REASON I'M EVEN STILL IN SCHOOL.

THE POONTANG?

MY *PARENTS*, IDIOT. I'VE BEEN LIVING UNDER THE DELUSION THAT IT'S POSSIBLE TO PLACATE THEM, AND IT'S OBVIOUSLY NOT.

I MEAN, I EVEN DRAGGED YOU TO CHURCH THAT TIME, AND IT DIDN'T COUNT FOR SHIT!

I COULD WORK MY ASS OFF, GET MY Ph.D., AND THEY'D STILL BE LIKE, "*YOU SHOULD'VE GONE MED SCHOOL! WHY YOU NOT MARRIED?*"

WHAT IS THIS... YOUR MARGARET CHO ROUTINE?

FUCK YOU. I'M SERIOUS.

SO YOUR SOLUTION IS TO JUST GIVE UP.

MAYBE.

I MEAN, AT LEAST *I'D* BE HAPPY. I DON'T GET WHY QUITTING IS ALWAYS EQUATED WITH FAILURE, WHEN REALLY—

OH SHIT.

WHAT?

ARE YOU FUCKING WITH ME?

GO

どこで食べようか？あの二階にある、
「ビレッジ横町」にする？

そうね。でもなんで
そんな風に私を見るの？

いや、君が
かわい過ぎて
目が離せないんだ。

I CAN'T BELIEVE SHE'D FALL FOR A FUCKING RICE KING. I CAN'T FUCKING BELIEVE IT.

AND WHAT DID HE DO...TAKE LANGUAGE CLASSES JUST SO HE COULD SCORE WITH JAPANESE GIRLS?

YEAH, I CAN IMAGINE HIM GOING TO CLASS AND BEING LIKE, "YEAH, YEAH...WHO CARES ABOUT THE DAYS OF THE WEEK. JUST TELL ME HOW TO SAY 'BLOW-JOB.'"

EW!

YEAH, SHUT UP!

WELL, I CAN SEE WHY YOU'RE ANGRY, BUT THERE'S NOTHING INHERENTLY WRONG WITH HAVING A "TYPE." I KNOW *I* CERTAINLY—

WELL, THIS IS FUCKING *DISGUSTING*, OKAY?

I MEAN, TELL ME YOU DON'T AGREE THAT WHEN YOU SEE A WHITE GUY WITH AN ASIAN GIRL, IT HAS CERTAIN...CONNOTATIONS.

AND WHEN YOU SEE AN ASIAN GUY WITH A WHITE GIRL, YOU THINK...?

GOOD FOR HIM! GOOD FOR BOTH OF THEM!

NOW YOU SEE WHY I LOVE THIS GUY?

I'M TRYING...

COME ON. YOU KNOW THERE'S SOMETHING CREEPY ABOUT A BIG WHITE GUY WHO'S HORNY FOR LITTLE, SKINNY ASIAN GIRLS.

I MEAN, WHAT DO YOU THINK *THAT'S* ABOUT?

WELL, IF YOU'RE IMPLYING AN UNDERCURRENT OF...WHAT? FETISHISM? PEDOPHILIA? THEN WHAT'S THE FLIP-SIDE OF THAT LINE OF THINKING?

IS YOUR ATTRACTION TO WHITE WOMEN A SUBLIMATED FORM OF ASSIMILATION?

ARE YOU TRYING TO ELEVATE YOUR-SELF IN SOCIETY'S EYES BY—

MAYBE!

JESUS...YOU DON'T HAVE TO TURN THIS INTO A PERSONAL ATTACK ON *ME!* I'M JUST...

NO, NO... I JUST THINK IT GETS A LITTLE...*DICEY* WHEN YOU START MAKING MORALISTIC GENERALIZATIONS BASED ON YOUR OWN WOUNDED EGO.

₹SIGH₹

AW...HE'S HAD A HARD DAY.

YOU'RE RIGHT. I'M NOT ATTACKING *YOU*, BEN.

LOOK...IF YOU DIG DEEP ENOUGH INTO ANYONE'S SEXUALITY, YOU'RE BOUND TO FIND SOMETHING YOU'D RATHER NOT EXAMINE TOO CLOSELY. BUT WHAT'S THE POINT IN PICKING IT APART? IT IS WHAT IT IS.

OKAY, PROFESSOR. SO LET'S NOT WORRY ABOUT ALL THE CHILD MOLESTERS AND RAPISTS IN THE WORLD BECAUSE "IT IS WHAT IT IS."

HE'S HAD TOO MUCH TO DRINK.

I KNOW FOR A FACT THAT HE ACTUALLY AGREES WITH YOU. HE'S JUST IN HIS OVER-THE-TOP CONTRARIAN MODE RIGHT NOW.

...AND IF YOU WANT TO FUCK SMALL ANIMALS, THAT'S OKAY, TOO, BECAUSE—

BEN.

LET ME JUST REMIND YOU THAT MEREDITH'S DAD IS WHITE AND HER MOM IS TAIWANESE.

BUT THAT'S BESIDE THE POINT.

YOU'RE ONLY HALF? HOW IS THAT BESIDE THE POINT?

BEN, I KNOW WHERE YOU'RE COMING FROM, BUT I THINK IT'S JUST A VERY SIMPLISTIC TAKE ON THINGS.

AND I DON'T WANT TO GET TOO PERSONAL HERE, BUT IT'S POSSIBLE THAT THIS GUY COULD BE IN LOVE WITH MIKO REGARDLESS OF RACE.

AND VICE-VERSA.

RIGHT.

THANK YOU FOR POINTING THAT OUT.

SO WHO WANTS ANOTHER DRINK?

PSSSSHHHH

DID YOU FUCK HER IN MY BED?

JESUS CHRIST!

WHAT THE *FUCK*, BEN? ARE YOU *CRAZY*?!

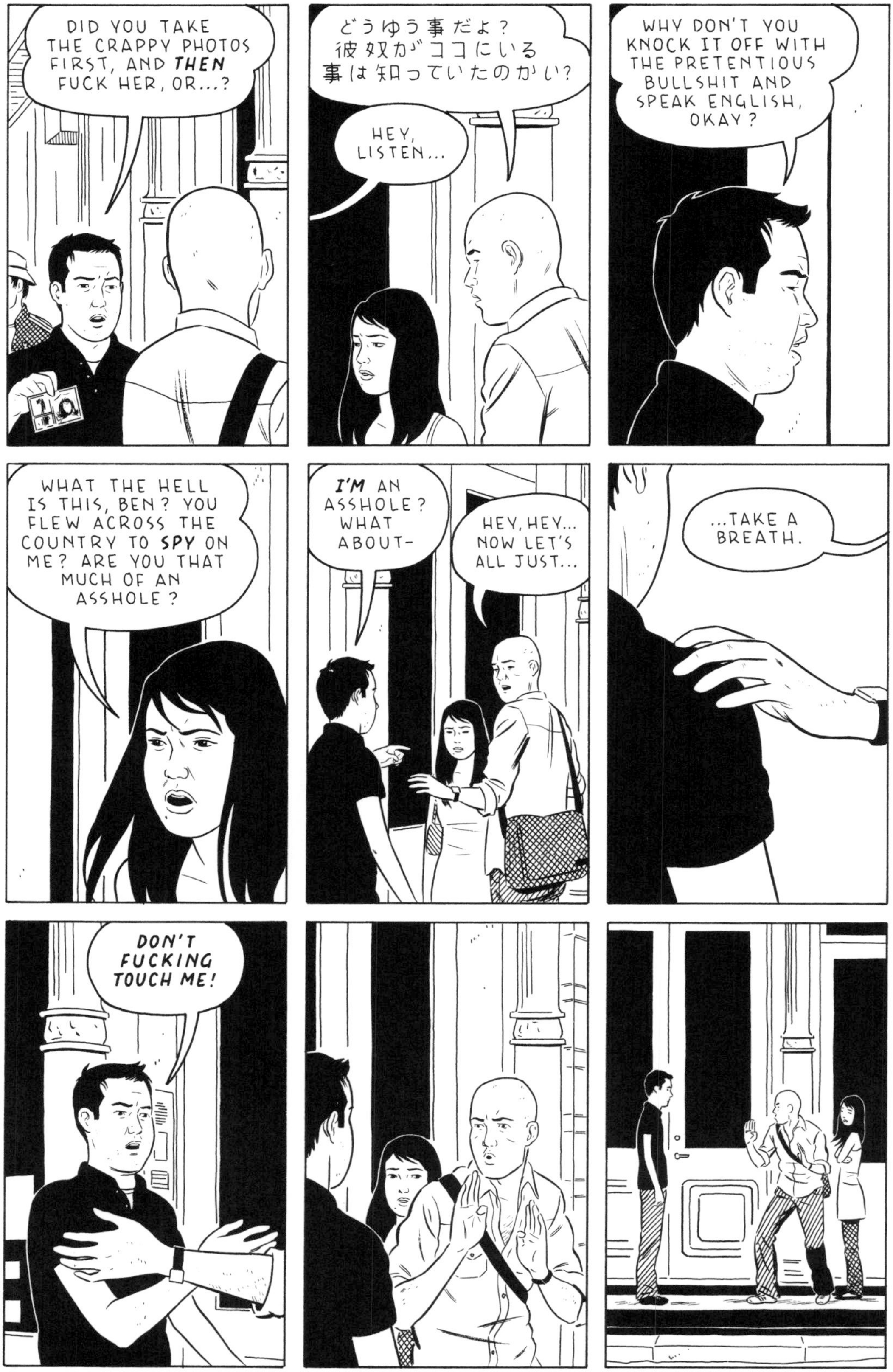
DID YOU TAKE THE CRAPPY PHOTOS FIRST, AND **THEN** FUCK HER, OR...?
どうゆう事だよ？ 彼奴がココにいる 事は知っていたのかい？
HEY, LISTEN...
WHY DON'T YOU KNOCK IT OFF WITH THE PRETENTIOUS BULLSHIT AND SPEAK ENGLISH, OKAY?
WHAT THE HELL IS THIS, BEN? YOU FLEW ACROSS THE COUNTRY TO **SPY** ON ME? ARE YOU THAT MUCH OF AN ASSHOLE?
I'M AN ASSHOLE? WHAT ABOUT-
HEY, HEY... NOW LET'S ALL JUST...
...TAKE A BREATH.
DON'T FUCKING TOUCH ME!

WHAT?

ARE YOU GONNA DO SOME *TAI CHI* ON ME?

JESUS, MIKO... YOU'RE CHEATING ON ME WITH THIS STEVEN SEAGAL *DIPSHIT*?

ENOUGH!

ALL RIGHT, LEON. LET ME JUST TALK TO HIM.

警察、呼ぼうか？

WHAT? NO. JUST...

JUST GO TO WORK, OKAY?

LET ME HANDLE THIS.

NICE TO MEET YOU!

SO, I'M GUESSING THIS IS *HIS* PLACE...?

YES.

NICE.

I CAN SEE HE REALLY LIKES HIS ORIENTAL ACCESSORIES.

SO YOU NEVER EVEN HAD YOUR OWN APARTMENT, HUH? DOES HE MAKE YOU PAY RENT, OR...?

COME ON, BEN. WHAT ARE YOU DOING HERE?

HANG ON... I'M STILL TRYING TO GET MY HEAD AROUND ALL THIS, YOU KNOW?

SO YOU BASIC- ALLY CAME OUT HERE TO BE WITH HIM, RIGHT? BUT I DON'T GET HOW YOU MET.

LET'S NOT GET INTO IT, OKAY? I OWE YOU AN APOLOGY, AND—

OH, WE'LL GET TO THAT.

BUT JUST... CLEAR THINGS UP A LITTLE FOR ME. HOW DOES ONE CROSS PATHS WITH A... *LEON CHRISTOPHER*?

...VISITING A FRIEND...

WHAT?

HE WAS VISITING A FRIEND WHO WORKED WITH ME AT THE FILM FESTIVAL.

WE MET FOR COFFEE A FEW TIMES, BUT... IT WAS NOTHING.

YOU'VE GOTTA STOP BULLSHITTING, MIKO. I THINK I CAN RECOGNIZE MY OWN FUCKING BED IN A PHOTO, OKAY?

WE TOOK A FEW PICTURES, BUT THAT'S IT. WE AGREED TO WAIT UNTIL I'D RESOLVED THINGS WITH YOU.

OH. SO... ARE YOU STILL "WAITING"?

BECAUSE *I* DON'T FEEL RESOLVED, DO YOU?

I GUESS I DIDN'T KNOW THAT "TAKING SOME TIME OFF" MEANT THAT YOU COULD *LIE* TO ME AND FUCK AROUND BEHIND MY BACK!

TCH...

LIKE *YOU'VE* BEEN SO HONEST AND DEVOTED...

WHAT'S *THAT* SUPPOSED TO MEAN?

IT MEANS MY FRIEND KOJI SAW YOU AT THE DURANT FOOD COURT HOLDING HANDS WITH SOME GIRL.

SHE SOUNDED LIKE JUST YOUR TYPE, TOO: YOUNG, BLONDE...

THAT'S FUCKING BULLSHIT.

YOU'VE ALWAYS BEEN PARANOID ABOUT THAT SHIT, BUT THIS IS A NEW LEVEL.

LOOK...I THINK IT'S OBVIOUS THAT THIS HAS BEEN A GOOD CHANGE FOR BOTH OF US.

I MEAN, WE WENT ABOUT IT IN A TOTALLY STUPID WAY, BUT...THIS ISN'T REALLY THE TIME TO RE-HASH ALL THAT.

YOU SHOULD'VE AT LEAST BEEN STRAIGHT WITH ME AND ENDED IT, INSTEAD OF DRAGGING IT OUT IN THIS NEBULOUS...

SIGH

DO YOU REMEMBER OUR LAST CONVER-SATION AT THE AIR-PORT, OR HAS YOUR SELECTIVE MEMORY BLOCKED THAT OUT?

YOU WERE IN ONE OF YOUR MOODS, AND I ASKED YOU TO SEND ME OFF ON A GOOD NOTE... SO THAT I'D HAVE A REASON TO WANT TO COME HOME.

AND DO YOU REMEMBER WHAT YOU DID?

YOU SAID, "THAT'S UP TO YOU" AND WALKED AWAY.

OH, SO THIS IS *MY* FAULT!

THAT'S GREAT.

THAT'S NOT THE POINT, BEN. I JUST THINK IT WAS TIME TO LET IT GO. FOR BOTH OF US.

BUT AREN'T YOU EMBARRASSED TO BE... *USED* LIKE THIS? THE MIKO *I* KNOW WOULD'VE RAKED THIS GIRL OVER THE COALS!

DON'T INSULT ME, BEN. I'M NOT BEING USED.

FINE.

BUT OF ALL THE PEOPLE TO...I MEAN, ARE YOU SERIOUS ABOUT THIS... RIDICULOUS, FAGGOTY WHITE GUY?

JESUS...

YOU DON'T KNOW HIM, OKAY?

AND IF IT REALLY MATTERS TO YOU, HE'S NOT WHITE.

ARE WE TALKING ABOUT THE SAME GUY?

HE'S HALF JEWISH, HALF NATIVE AMERICAN.

OH...THAT'S HILARIOUS!

IS THAT WHAT HE PUT ON HIS COLLEGE APPLICATION?

OR WAIT... DO THEY EVEN *HAVE* AFFIRMATIVE ACTION IN FASHION SCHOOL?

YOU SHOULD PROBABLY GO NOW.

SURE. BUT JUST OUT OF CURIOSITY... HOW'S THE INTERNSHIP GOING?

IT'S FINE.

MY COUSIN WILL CALL YOU AT SOME POINT ABOUT PICKING UP THE REST OF MY STUFF.

YOU KNOW...WE'VE HAD OUR ISSUES IN THE PAST, BUT I ALWAYS THOUGHT YOU WERE BASICALLY AN HONEST, GOOD PERSON.

I GUESS I'VE BEEN A FUCKING IDIOT ALL ALONG.

BEN, WAIT...

I SHOULD'VE BEEN MORE DIRECT WITH YOU A LONG TIME AGO, AND I APOLOGIZE FOR NOT DOING THAT.

BUT EVEN AT MY MOST FRUSTRATED, I FELT A LOT OF SYMPATHY FOR YOU. AND THAT'S HOW YOU BASICALLY KEPT ME TRAPPED FOR THE LAST TWO YEARS.

"TRAPPED"? DON'T TRY TO PLAY THE VICTIM NOW, MIKO. IT'S FUCKING PATHETIC.

YOU KNOW WHAT'S PATHETIC, BEN? TRYING TO HOLD ONTO SOMETHING JUST BECAUSE YOU'RE PATHOLOGICALLY AFRAID OF CHANGE.

SO THAT'S MY BIG CRIME, HUH? I DON'T JUST *GIVE UP*? OOH, GOSH... WHAT A *MONSTER* I AM!

≤SIGH≥

I THINK YOU ALSO HAVE A PROBLEM WITH DEPRESSION AND ANGER MANAGEMENT... WEIRD SELF-HATRED ISSUES... AND JUST THE *RELENTLESS* NEGATIVITY...

WHAT ABOUT YOU, MIKO? IF YOU COULD *JUST ONCE* BE THAT ANALYTICAL ABOUT YOURSELF, YOU'D—

LET ME FINISH.

YOU'RE CRITICAL OF EVERYTHING, YOU HAVE NO CAREER AMBITIONS ANYMORE, YOU HAVE... WHAT? ONE FRIEND?

OKAY...

AND LET'S JUST BE HONEST, BEN. YOU'D RATHER *WHACK OFF* TO SOME BARBIE-DOLL *SLUTS* ON TV THAN—

ARE YOU DONE?

ARE YOU DONE WITH THE FUCKING RATIONALIZING, OR ARE YOU GONNA

THAT'S ENOUGH.

I'M CLOSING THE DOOR NOW, BEN.

OKAY, WAIT.

WE BOTH NEED TO JUST... CALM DOWN. THIS IS WHAT HAPPENS: WE GET CAUGHT UP IN THE ARGUMENT, AND—

BEN.

DON'T DO THIS TO ME.

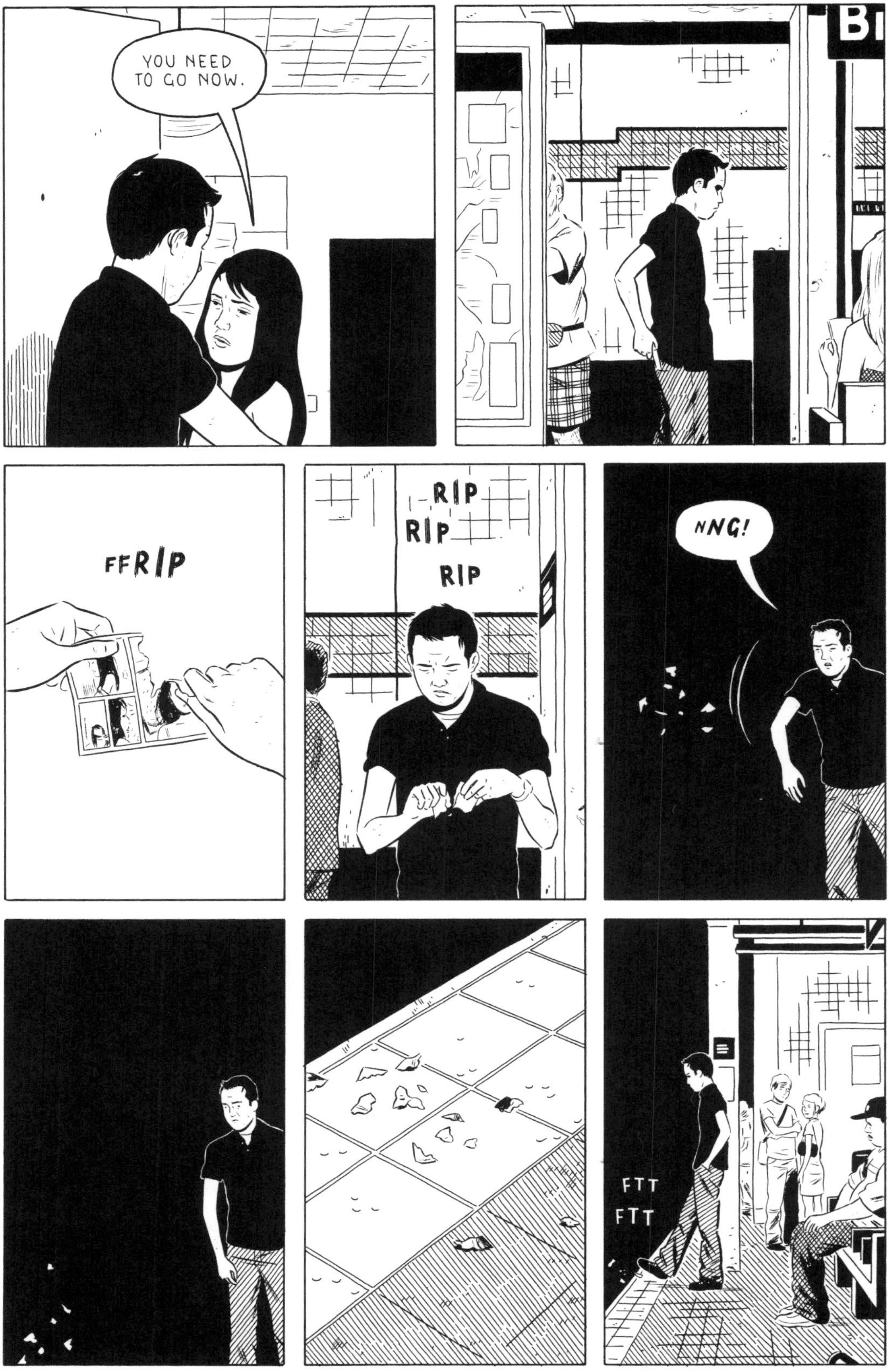
YOU NEED TO GO NOW.
FFRIP
RIP
RIP
RIP
NNG!
FTT
FTT

Since 1931

I JUST WANTED TO SAY "THANKS" TO EVERYONE FOR BEING HERE.

I DON'T KNOW IF TURNING THIRTY-TWO IS REALLY SOMETHING TO *CELEBRATE*, BUT I WILL STILL ALLOW YOU TO BUY ME DRINKS.

HA HA HA

UM... LAST MONTH I HAD THE GOOD FORTUNE OF CROSSING PATHS WITH AN OLD ACQUAINTANCE WHO WAS VISITING FROM CALIFORNIA...

AND I DON'T THINK IT'S ANY SECRET THAT I'VE SINCE FALLEN... HEAD OVER HEELS FOR HER.

SHE'S FALLING-DOWN DRUNK!

HA HA HA

AND JUST A FEW MINUTES AGO, SHE TOLD ME THAT SHE'S DECIDED TO MOVE HERE, AND THAT'S ABOUT THE BEST BIRTHDAY PRESENT I COULD IMAGINE.

CLAP CLAP CLAP CLAP CLA

SO KEEP BUYING ME DRINKS, BUT BUY ALICE A DRINK, TOO, AND WELCOME HER TO HER NEW HOME!

CLAP CLAP CLAP CLA

CLAP CLAP CLAP CLAP CLAP

CLAP CLAP CLAP CLA

105

THERE YOU ARE!

OH...I WAS JUST GONNA GO BACK TO THE APARTMENT AND GET PACKED UP. I'VE GOT AN EARLY FLIGHT...

I'M NOT MOVING JUST FOR HER, YOU KNOW.

WHATEVER HAPPENS, I'LL STILL BE IN THE GREATEST CITY IN THE WORLD.

RIGHT.

I GUESS IF YOU'RE INTO HUMIDITY, RUDE-NESS, RATS, MUGGINGS, TERRORIST ATTACKS...

RIGHT... AND BERKELEY IS **PERFECT**...

I MEAN, WHAT'S KEEP-ING YOU THERE? I'LL BE BACK NEXT MONTH TO GET MY STUFF. START PLANNING NOW... WE CAN SHARE A U-HAUL!

TCH...I CAN'T MOVE 3,000 MILES TO BE WITH SOMEONE I'M NOT HAVING INTERCOURSE WITH.

BESIDES, YOU WON'T BE GONE LONG. I GIVE THIS... THREE MONTHS, TOPS.

AH...THE OLD BEN TANAKA PEP-TALK!

YOU KNOW, THERE'S STILL A PART OF ME THAT THINKS WHEN I LAND IN OAKLAND, EVERYTHING WILL JUST BE...BACK TO NORMAL.

THE THEATER WILL BE OPEN...YOU'LL BE BACK IN SCHOOL... MIKO WILL BE WAIT-ING FOR ME AT THE AIRPORT...

WELL, LUCKY FOR YOU, THAT'S NOT THE CASE. I KNOW IT'S HARD FOR YOU TO SEE THE BRIGHT SIDE OF THINGS, BUT...

I MEAN, *NOW* AM I FINALLY ALLOWED TO TALK SHIT ABOUT HER? FUCKING TWO-FACED BITC

NO, DON'T.

LOOK... WE ALL HAVE OUR REASONS.

TAP TAP

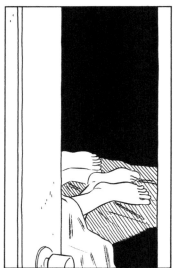

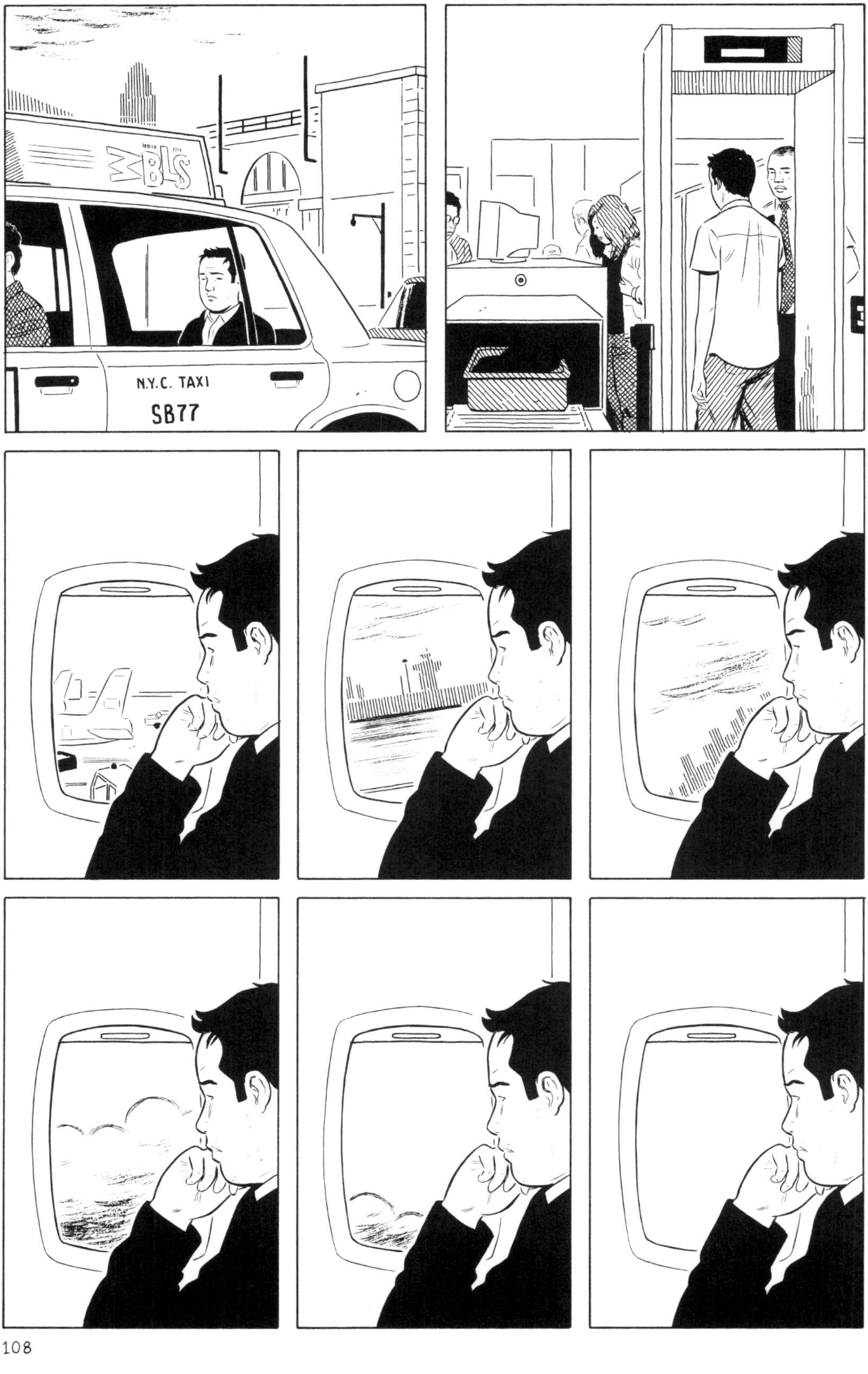
WBLS
N.Y.C. TAXI
SB77

ACKNOWLEDGMENTS

Thank you: Sarah Brennan, Peggy Burns, cartoonist pals, Tom
Devlin, Naomi Hyon, Sonjia Hyon, John Kuramoto, Taro Nettleton,
Chris Oliveros, Jamie Quail, Daniel Raeburn, Rebecca Rosen.